# JUST FINISH THE RACE:

## A Mother's Journey *to* Finish Her Son's Race

## LAURIE LEE

*Photo by: Les Duggins, USC-Upstate*

*In loving memory of Our Josh—*
*You loved everyone unconditionally*
*You laughed continuously*
*You just plain LIVED!*

# CONTENTS

# ACKNOWLEDGMENTS

An accident on 4th Street in Spartanburg, SC changed a community, brought unity to a college campus, and forever changed the dynamics of four families. There will never be enough words of gratitude to express to the three young gentlemen who heroically pulled my son from a fiery accident and who also attempted to save three fellow classmates, teammates, a best friend, and total strangers without even thinking twice about their own safety. Sam, Andrew, and Micah you are the definition of a hero; humble and kind who genuinely cares for others.

I give God all the glory because He let Johnny and me be Josh's parents. We have learned that there are no coincidences in life. Everything does happen for a reason. We had Josh only 20 years but Josh will forever live in our hearts because of Him.

To Johnny, we lost something that no one can ever comprehend because Josh was our Josh. We have grown as Christians but mostly as a couple. We see life differently now. You have allowed me to cry and talk about Josh because you truly know my heartache and pain. I love you more than words can ever detail. We will see our baby boy again. This is our race now and I know we both will finish it for him.

To my daughter Macy, you have shown tremendous courage and strength to maintain your goals of pursuing your dreams. Josh was not just your brother but a best friend. You two made us proud every day and we are honored to be called your parents. The love your dad and I have for you two cannot ever be measured.

To my immediate family and close friends, all of you truly know the heartache Johnny and I face on a daily basis without our Josh by our sides. Without everyone's support and a shoulder to cry on we would have not made it through this past year.

Dr. Bill Westafer, I cannot thank you enough for being our unwavering guide and mostly a friend through our journey of loss.

To Courtney, Josh loved you with all his heart and soul. You were his soulmate, his best friend, and the love of his life. You never tried to change Josh. You let Josh be Josh. For that alone, Johnny and I are grateful. We love you dearly and forever will.

To all of the 911 communicators, first responders, South Carolina Highway policeman, Spartanburg Regional Trauma team and Surgical-Trauma unit nurses and Chaplins, Spartanburg County Coroner's office, and Dunbar Funeral Home. Thank you so much for your compassion and grace during the tragic loss of our Josh.

To Dr. James Scardo, Dr. Stephen Vermillion, Dr. M. Ryan Laye and my fellow coworkers at MGC Maternal Fetal Medicine all of you held my heart and grieved along aside of me. All of you see my heartache on a daily basis. Having a shoulder to cry on when I look upon the room Josh died in, to just receiving a much needed hug because all of you can see the pain written on my face. For this alone I will be eternally grateful.

To Tammy Whaley and the University of South Carolina Upstate administration, faculty, classmates, coaches, and especially fellow athletes, thank you so much for the love and support you have shown over the loss of everyone's Josh. The loss of Josh, Mills, James, and Sarah will always be remembered by their legacies and their mark they left on everyone's heart. We will and forever are SpartanStrong.

To all whom helped get my book published: through your generosity Johnny and I are truly blessed to know there are still angels who walk among us. Love to you all.

# THERE IS A TREE THAT RESIDES ON 4TH STREET

There is a tree that resides on 4th street.
With his branches stretching high into the sky.
His leaves swaying with the breeze on a crisp autumn night.
Enjoying the mist sprinkling its moisture on to him while he sleeps.

There is a tree that resides on 4th street.
Who was awakening from his sleep?
It was five USC Upstate athletes.
Then the tree looked down and began to weep.
For he knew his shade would be forever covering hallowed ground.

There is a tree that resides on 4th street.
Who saw our Lord and Savior come and kneel beneath?
Four precious souls were now the Lord's to keep.
The Lord called each by name: Joshua, James, Mills, and Sara it is
time to follow me home.

There is a tree that resides on 4th street.
As day approached and voices could be heard.
As friends and family cried and laid flowers, teddy bears, tennis
shoes, and cleats at the trees feet.
There was a green ribbon and bow now fastened around his chest.
The tree wore it proud and true because that ribbon is now a re-
membrance of what happened while he slept.

There is a tree that resides on 4th street.
For now he is forever scarred.
As the trees foliage begins to fall he is reminded of what took place
in that churchyard.
For he is now forever standing guard.

# CHAPTER ONE

*The Phone Call That Changes Our Lives*

Aphone ringing in the middle of the night is never to deliver good news. Johnny and I wake to a ringing cell phone at 3:30 a.m. on October 11, 2015. Johnny's mom wasn't feeling well so we both expect his sister Lisa or his mom to be on the other end of the phone. They weren't. It is Tammy Whaley. That one phone call forever changes our lives as we know it.

Tammy is a long-term customer at White's Pine Street Exxon where Johnny works, but mostly she is a close friend. She is also the assistant vice chancellor for university communications and the media contact at the University of South Carolina Upstate (USC Upstate) where our 20-year-old son Josh attends college. Josh, a physical education major, runs cross-country/track.

"Why is Tammy calling so early?" I ask Johnny, thinking she was having car trouble or that Mr. Junie White was sick

– he is the owner of White's Pine Street Exxon where Johnny has worked for 35 years. He is also the closest thing to a father that Johnny ever had because Johnny's daddy died when he was two-weeks-old from a massive heart attack at the age of 28.

"Are you at the hospital?" Tammy asks Johnny.

"No, should we be?" Johnny replies.

Tammy is calling to tell us that Josh had been involved in a serious car accident and that we need to get to the hospital as soon as possible.

We both scramble to get dressed. From a closet filled with clothes, I chose the green, three-quarter length sleeve top, jeans and my black Danskos. Johnny quickly dressed in a tee shirt, jeans and his tennis shoes. I run upstairs to wake up our daughter Macy who dresses in less than a minute in her normal sweats, tee shirt, and tennis shoes. Just like her dad she doesn't care what she wears.

Johnny is waiting in his truck when Macy and I rush out in the rain and fog. I think it has been foggy and raining for three weeks. Just as we leave home Johnny gets a call from Mr. White who is actually driving to our house.

"Tammy called me and said Josh has been in an accident and it is serious. Are you headed to the hospital?" asks Mr. White.

"Yes, we are," says Johnny.

I can hear Mr. White saying that Tammy has called him in an effort to reach us because the hospital has been calling our home since 2 a.m. I began questioning why in the world the hospital called Tammy instead of us. We would learn three weeks later that the rain had shorted out our land line.

"I will meet you there," Mr. White tells Johnny.

Once again I began questioning, "Why Tammy?" Then it hit me. She handles media relations and crisis communications at USC Upstate. My heart sinks to my feet.

Johnny keeps saying, "I knew something was going to

happen to him. Laurie, I have felt this all day, all day!"

"I called Josh all day asking where he was and if he needed anything. Remember, we went by the station (where Josh works for his dad part-time) to check on him. I have had this feeling all day that something was going to happen to him."

I began praying, "Please Lord let my baby be alright. Please let our Josh be alright."

Johnny tells me he talked to Josh around 10:30 p.m. Josh told him he was eating a hot dog and was "just chilling." Josh always says this – it is his way of saying he is home and in for the night. Josh has to be up at 5:30 a.m. every day to run with the cross country team. We know Josh wouldn't be up this late at night especially when he has to run the next morning.

My mind races just as fast as Johnny drives up Pine Street. This just doesn't make sense.

Sam Cheshier, Josh's best friend and a USC Upstate soccer player, is standing in the emergency room entrance when we pull up. Josh and Sam have been friends since middle school. They were two of a kind. Where you saw Josh you saw Sam. Whenever these two were around you would be constantly laughing. That was just Josh and Sam, always cutting up.

"Is Josh conscious, Sam?" I ask.

"They will not tell me anything," Sam replies.

At the entrance desk stands a chaplain who greets us.

"We are Joshua Lee's parents. We were told he was brought in from an accident. Can we see him please?" I say.

"Can you follow me to the consult room?" says the chaplain.

I begin crying and refuse to go with her. Being a nurse I know what it means to be taken to the consult room. I am bound and determined not to go in there because nothing but bad news was going to follow.

"Josh was involved in a serious car accident and is in the trauma-surgical intensive care unit," she tells us. "Three of

Josh's fellow student-athletes have been killed in the accident and are still at the scene."

I am still praying, "Please let my baby be ok, please!"

Johnny and I hold hands while Macy follows us to the intensive care unit where Tammy greets us. I can tell she has been crying.

She hugs us and Johnny asks, "What happened Tammy?"

"Josh, along with four other students, were on their way to Cookout Restaurant around 1:30 a.m. when they hit a tree on 4th Street in Boiling Springs," she says.

This is one mile from Joshua's apartment. I know at that moment that Josh is badly hurt. Still I am praying, "Please, please Lord let my baby be ok!"

The chaplain leads us to another consult room within the intensive care unit waiting room. Other USC Upstate personnel are arriving to the unit and I notice that several family members sleeping in the waiting area are waking up due to commotion. I call both my sisters, Tammy Jordan and April Clark, but their phones go straight to voicemail. I can't think of their home numbers. I call my mom and she answers on the second ring.

It's now 4:20 a.m. and I say between tears, "Mama, Josh has been in a bad wreck. It is bad Mama, it's really bad."

"Let me call Tammy and April and we will be there shortly," she tells me.

Johnny talks with his sister Lisa Davidson and she is on her way too. His mom, Jo Lee, lives alone and doesn't handle sickness or death well, so we wait to call her until we learn more.

So now the waiting game begins.

## WE CRIED

We cried when we got the phone call.
We cried because we had to let you go.
We cried because we had to pick out your grave.
We cried because we had to choose your casket.
We cried planning your funeral.
We cried when the hearse took you to your final resting place.
We cried as they took us away.
We cried as we randomly smell your cologne.
We cried when we saw your name or see your signature.
We cried when your favorite song comes on the radio.
We cried at each passing day knowing you are really gone.
We cried because we were so blessed to know that you are a
Heavenly Angel.
We cried and begged God to tell us why?
The day we see you again our sweet child
We will cry.

## FROM A FATHERS HEART

I was there the day you were born.
I was the first to hold you son.
I was told you looked like me.
I was proud as can be.
I was there to tell you goodnight.
I was there for every baseball, football, and wrestling match.
I was always there to see you run.

I taught you what was right from wrong.
I taught you how to be strong.
I taught you how to love.
I taught you how to drive.
I also taught you how to always give hundred percent.

I was proud the day you graduated.
I was proud the day you started USC Upstate.
I was proud of the man you became.
I was proud to call you my Son.

Now that you are gone I have cried so hard.
Now that you are gone I feel all alone.
Now that you are gone I have nothing but heartache.
Now that you are gone I am trying to be strong.

My son I make this solemn vow I will never forget you.
My son I made sure your legacy will forever live on.
My son till the day I see again I will live through your eyes.
My son these words are from your father's heart.
My son I loved you unconditionally from the start.

# CHAPTER TWO

## *The News That Our Son is Going to Die*

It is now 4:30 on Sunday morning and Johnny, Macy, Mr. White and I are waiting for the doctors to come into the blasted consult room, in the intensive care unit, to tell us some news—any news—on our Josh. A knock at the door alerts us that all the physicians, nurses and the chaplain are here to tell us about Josh's medical condition. I am sitting across from Mr. White with Macy beside me and Johnny to my left. The first to enter the room are the surgeons on the trauma team. They introduce themselves but all I hear is "TRAUMA."

The lead trauma surgeon tells us that Josh has sustained severe chest trauma and is on a ventilator to help him breathe. Josh is having a hard time keeping his oxygen levels up. He also has bilateral chest tubes to keep his lungs inflated and drained because of the trauma and bruising to his lungs. Multiple blood transfusions are necessary because of the massive blood loss he sustained.

Johnny, Macy and I are still praying, "Please let Josh be okay! Please!"

The second doctor speaks up and introduces himself as the neurosurgeon. Right then and there I panic.

"Your son has sustained a traumatic head injury," he begins to tell me but I stop him in mid-sentence and ask with tears flowing down my cheeks, "Is our Josh brain dead?"

The neurosurgeon replies in a somber voice, "Yes ma'am he is but, Joshua's brain stem is still functioning right now." He also says that our Josh is not going to make it.

I lose it right there and grab Johnny. We hold each other and cry. I beg Johnny not to let God take our baby. "Please Johnny! Please don't let Him take our Josh!"

The neurosurgeon asks if we want to see Josh and simultaneously without hesitation we both reply, "Yes."

Macy is holding my hand and crying. Mr. White is teary as he tells the nurses who take us back to see our Josh, "I am the grandfather and I'm coming with them."

At 4:45 a.m. we finally get to room seven in the surgical/trauma intensive care unit. Behind the striped curtain is my baby boy. My Josh, our Josh who is fighting for his life.

Before we go in the nurses tell us not to touch the back of Josh's head and to be gentle when we touch his face because of the facial fractures.

"What facial fractures?" I ask as the image of Josh's face mangled and his head collapsed enter my mind. But, I am still praying, "God please help us do this and not to take my baby. Please!"

The nurse draws back the curtain and lying there motionless is our Josh. The only noise we hear are the machines working, as diligently as they can, to pump fluids, blood, and oxygen into our son. I walk to the right side of Josh and Johnny walks to Josh's left. Macy is at Josh's legs behind me. Mr. White is behind Johnny. The nurses explain to us about all the tubes and wires and what they meant. I know exactly what they mean and why they are there. Johnny didn't so it helped him some. As his mother I want to cradle my baby and tell him he will be alright. But, as a nurse I know my baby is never coming home again. I ask the nurses, "Is my baby in pain?" They reply, "No ma'am, he is not."

I touch my baby on his forehead and say, "We here Josh, we are here baby." No movement, nothing. I inspected every part of my son, our Josh. I notice two intravenous lines going with blood being pumped into his broken body. Josh's endotracheal tube is moving and his chest is rising with every pump of breath he is receiving by a machine. He has a gash on his chin that has been stapled. He has bilateral chest tubes with drainage falling into the reservoirs. He has a gash on his right foot that has also been stapled. He has a catheter in place, too. Josh has some bruising around his left eye but, nothing like my mind was telling me beforehand.

Josh is cold when I touch my baby's chest. I want warmth for him. I can't comprehend why Josh is so cold. Then I realize it. He isn't getting oxygen to his body. I notice the nurses coming in two by two every few minutes and pushing intravenous medications through my son's IV lines. I know these medications are to help control and regulate Josh's vital signs. They are trying desperately to sustain his life.

Johnny and Macy stand there as I inspect my child. I gently rub his face and he has blood coming from his nose, ears and the back of his head. I rub his forehead and feel my baby's head injuries. I lost it. Johnny begins to plea bargain with God, "Please Lord, take me! Take me! Don't take Josh. Take Me!"

I have known Johnny for 30 years and I have never seen him pray and plea with anyone until now. We both pray and plea for God not to take our Josh. Not our Josh.

I beg Josh to open his eyes and talk to Mama. Talk to us son. Please baby! Still there is no response from Josh, no movement from him at all. Quietness and the machines working are all we hear. I kiss my baby on his cheeks and wipe away the blood from his mouth and nose. I hold my Josh. It is my responsibility to take care of my baby, our Josh.

The nurse returns and presses Josh's wallet into Johnny's hand. "This was all that was on his person at the time of arrival to the ICU unit," she says. I know Josh never goes anywhere without his cell phone and the watch his girlfriend Courtney Reilly gave him. Never!

I leave Josh for a short period of time to see if my mom, sisters, and Lisa are at the hospital yet. It is now 5:15 a.m. and I share the news of the car accident and Josh's condition with my mother, sisters, brother-in-laws Mark Jordan and Terry Clark, and Lisa. They want to go see Josh but, out of the corner of my eye I notice several the USC Upstate personnel and Sandy Sandago, the athletic trainer, standing off to the right.

I know Courtney needs to get here to say her goodbyes to Josh but she is in Florida with the USC Upstate women's soccer team. I walk up and they ask me about Josh's condition. I tell them that Josh has been pronounced brain dead but he still has brain stem activity. I tell them that because of his chest injuries, Josh will not make it.

I look at Tammy, Sandy, and Chancellor Tom Moore and say, "Josh's girlfriend plays soccer for you and she is in Florida at a tournament. Please get her home now."

Within minutes Tammy tells me that Courtney's coach is telling her that Josh has been in a car accident and she needs to come home. Courtney, who will be put on a plane within an hour, is not being told that Josh won't survive. She should arrive back in Spartanburg by mid - afternoon.

I return to my family to prepare them for Josh's injuries and tell them what to expect when they see him. They all touch Josh and tell him how much they love him. All the while I was rubbing my Josh's forehead, telling him, "It is okay. We are here. Please open your eyes son, please!"

I leave my family at Josh's bedside with Macy still hugging her brother's legs not wanting to let go of him. It is okay. He is and will always be her brother. I find Johnny and he is crying and I tell him over and over, "Please don't let Him take Josh!" "Please Johnny; don't let Him take our Josh!"

"I wish I could Laurie. I would take his place in a minute," he tells me with tears streaming down his face. We stand there holding one another knowing we are losing our only son. Our Josh.

It is 5:45 a.m. now and I know that we have to call our best friends to be by our sides. We are all family. We go on every vacation together. We eat out every weekend. I call Angie Bryson first to let her know Josh is badly injured from a car accident and is in intensive care. She says, 'We are on the way." I ask Angie her to call her mom, "Ms. Shelia" Kline is a Godly woman and has a direct line with Him with her amen corner. I call Jennifer Dodd and tell her the same. Johnny calls his long time childhood friend Jeff Wyatt. All the families are at our side within 30 minutes. Angie, Frankie, Nick, his girlfriend Makayla, Steve Jones, Jennifer, Ashley and Taylor Jones, Jeff and Mandy Wyatt are with us.

I go back to be with Josh. Johnny is going back and forth. Angie and Jennifer follow me back at one time. I feel like I am floating on a breeze. I am oblivious to my surroundings. All that matters to me is my son. I am his mother and I am the one who should be taking care of him. Macy stays with me and continues to hug her brother's legs.

I ask for some alcohol pads or cloth to clean Josh's face. I want to rid him of all the blood and drainage that had dried upon his beautiful face. I didn't know at the time because I am oblivious to what people are telling me but a nurse tells me not to rub hard because of his injuries. I am his mother and I will clean my baby's face. I clean every inch of his face -- gently and preciously because my heart knows this is the last time I will care for my Josh. I investigate and clean every inch of Josh. I want to remember every cell of his face. It's my responsibility, as his mother, to take care of him. There are a few places that I can't reach but I have enough knowledge to know not to move him.

The sun is up and shining so brightly as 7 a.m. nears. It is like God lifted the gloom that is surrounding us and brought the feeling of calm and peace into our presence. I sit with my mom and sisters. My brother-in-law Terry and Lisa have brought Johnny's mom, Jo, to the hospital. She won't go see him because of Josh's injuries. I see our other longtime friends Jeff and Nicole Crocker walk in and she is crying. Also, Crystal, Brian, and Shannon Jones are here and I notice Johnny's aunt and uncle Nancy & Harold Richards too. I begin to feel sick and escape to the restroom. The nausea and gut wrenching pain won't subside. My sister April brings me some water and it helps. More of our friends, Todd and Sarah Justus, arrive. I see that Sam is still here and I take him back to see Josh.

Once back at Josh's bedside, I gently rub Josh's forehead and tell him softly, "We love you son." Johnny and Macy were at the bedside, too. Sam drops to his knees and cries over Josh. He is losing his best friend. I start crying again and try to comfort Sam. Sam is, and always forever be, our second son.

Sam and the other two good Samaritans (Andrew Richards and Micah Burnett) came upon the car crash and saved our Josh. They got Josh out of the car before it caught on fire. Johnny and I will be forever grateful to them but, mostly to Sam. Sam already has a place in our hearts but, his heroic actions he endured, to save everyone's Josh, confirming his place within our family. I vow to one day meet the two men who helped Sam get Josh out of that car. One day!

## ONE MORE DAY

God gave me you only for just a little awhile.
If I only had one more day.
One more day to hear your laugh.
One more day to see your smile.
One more day for you to call my name.
On more day of your random burst into song.
One more day of your endless aggravating antics.
One more day to have your bear hugs.
One more day to look into your baby blues.
One more day to hear I love you too Mama.
One more day to gaze upon your beautiful face.
One more day to tell you how so proud we are of you.
One more day to just tell you I love you son.
If we only had one more day.

## LET GO

I will not forget you.
I will not let you go.
I'm grasping, holding on tight. Hang on son hang on.
I will not let go.
Stay with us son. Stay here son. Please don't go.
You are needed here with us.
I'm still grasping, holding on tight.
I will not let you go.
Your laughter still needs to be heard.
Your smile still needs to be enjoyed.
Your everlasting love still needs to be felt.
I'm still grasping, holding on tight.
I will not let you go.
Decisions? Decisions?
I don't want to let go. I just can't. Please God!
Please don't take him.
I'm grasping, holding on tight.
I will not let you go.
Stop! Stop! Let go son. Let go.
It's ok baby, let go.
Slower his heart beats.
He is gone.
I love you baby!
Please God take care of my baby.
But, I'm grasping, will forever hold on tight.
I will never let you go.

# CHAPTER THREE
## *To Let Our Josh Go*

It's 7:30 a.m. when the nurses call us into another consult room. Yes, another blasted consult room. She says the doctors are on the way to talk to us about Josh's condition. The doctors arrive and tell us that they have used all means necessary to maintain Josh's breathing. They also have exceeded the maximum dosage of medication available to them.

The nurses escort Johnny, Macy and me back into Josh's room. Once back at his bedside the doctor says, "Josh is unable to oxygenate his blood to maintain his heart to keep beating. Do you want us to begin CPR once his heart stops or do you want us to remove him from life support?"

I am crying again and I turn to look at Johnny who is tearful also. All Johnny can do is to shake his head no. I know that means no more. Let my Josh, our Josh, go. We are losing my baby within minutes and Josh will suffer no more.

It is now around 8:00 a.m. on a sunny Sunday morning and I think of the irony. I gave birth to Josh on Sunday, August 13, 1995 at 8:20 a.m. Now, on October 11, 2015, Johnny, Macy and I hold our Josh and watch as he takes his last breath here on Earth.

The nurses come in and disconnect all his IV's. One nurse turns off the ventilator and disconnects the tubing but, the endotracheal tube has to remain. They give Johnny, Macy and me a chair to sit beside Josh. I am rubbing his forehead again, making sure I touch every inch of precious face, to remember every inch of him. All of a sudden Josh bucks and tenses up to the left. His right leg bends up towards his body. Bloody fluid begins pouring out of his endotracheal tube. Johnny jumps backwards and so does Macy. I cry out, "What is happening to my baby?"

The nurses rush into the room. One nurse uses the suction to clear the tube and the other nurse says she has permission to remove the tube. Again I ask, "What caused him to do this? If Josh was brain dead how did he tense up and reflex like he did?"

According to the nurses, when someone is dying their body will release pressure. Since Josh was on a ventilator, his body has to release that pressure. It still didn't help matters to see Josh do that. Another nurse enters the room and pushes some pain medications that will ease his breathing. I know it is to give him an easier transition into death. I remain at Josh's head, rubbing his forehead and hair. I tell Josh, "It is okay son, let go. Let go baby. It is okay." Johnny holds Josh's hand and Macy is still holding his legs.

With my hand on his forehead I watch the heart monitor. I am attentively watching Josh's heartbeat get slower and slower. At 8:06 on a sunny, Sunday morning on October 11, 2015 my Josh, our Josh, takes his last breath. He is peaceful.

Two nurses confirm that Josh has no heartbeat and the doctor calls the time of death. Once the doctor calls out, "Time of death, 8:06 a.m.," I grab my son's face and kiss and kiss him. I cry, crying for my baby. My baby, my Josh is gone. Johnny and Macy cry as loudly as I do.

I look up and realize that my office is directly across the corridor from where my beloved son, Josh has just died. How in the world am I going to be able to work and look out the window every day and see this exact room day in and day out? I can't! I can't do it, period!

The nurses let us stay with Josh for about 10 minutes before we have to step out for the coroner investigators to examine Josh. Macy has worked as a coroner's investigator before and explains to us that Josh is now considered a fatality in a motor vehicle accident. Our Josh is now labeled a statistics in the book of motor vehicle accidents. We kiss and tell Josh goodbye and we all sob as we leave his side. My baby boy, our Josh just died!

Johnny, Macy and I walked out of the ICU corridor and I notice several nurses who are crying. Me being me went right up to them and hugged them as they wept. They kept repeating, "I am so sorry, so sorry." I replied, "It is okay. Thank you for giving such good and compassionate care to my baby." I notice the coroner's investigators at the desk and my heart just breaks all over again because I fear they are not going to let me see my baby anymore.

Walking back to the unit, we meet Dr. Bill Westafer who has been our pastor at Cowpens First Baptist Church since 2009. No, we haven't attended church regularly but Preacher Bill is here for us and loves us unconditionally. Seeing his presence, at our time of need, eases our pain just a little. We explain to him that Josh has just passed away and the coroner investigators are with him now. "I was there when my son took his first breath but, never would I have imagined that I would be there when he took his last. My Josh, our Josh is gone," I tell Preacher Bill. We also tell him that Josh was in motor vehicle accident at 1:45 a.m. with four of his friends and fellow student-athletes, three of whom perished in the fire.

I realize for the first time that my Josh, our Josh, was spared. I feel this deep achiness within my heart for the other parents and I began praying for them along with our preacher. Johnny and I had the chance to touch Josh and to tell Josh goodbye. The other parents who lost their children in this crash will never get to touch or see their child ever again. My heart breaks and bleeds for them.

# JOSHUA'S PRAYER

I am praying for all of you.
Please don't shed anymore tears for me.
I know you don't understand why God took me home so soon.
I am with you in spirit day and night.
I promise everything will be alright.
I am praying for all of you.
I pray for all you to receive some peace
For my heart will always be yours to keep.
I am praying for all of you.
I will check on all of you from time to time.
Just look for my signs that I am near.
For you know it will bring all of you laughter instead of tears.
I am praying for all of you.
I am now an angel of God.
I have the greatest blessing of them all.
For my love for all of you will always remain the same.
I am praying for all of you.
Jesus called my name, grabbed my hand, and said, "Well done
my child, well done!" Now follow me home.
So when it's your time to go I promise I will be first in line.
For after you see the Lord you will see me.
For I have always loved you my friends but especially my family.
Gone
My baby is gone
But, never forgotten.
My baby boy no longer laughs here on Earth.
But, his laughter is forever heard amongst the Angels of God.

My child of mine can no longer run the grassy hills of USC Upstate.
But, he can soar with the Eagles above the mountain tops.
My son can no longer give us a much needed hug.
But, he is forever embraced in the arms of God.
My son can never again kiss us goodnight.
But, he has been blessed by God's amazing grace.
My son, my baby boy's heart will no longer beat.
But, he was saved by Jesus's mercy and my son will
always live on in our hearts.
My baby is gone.

# CHAPTER FOUR
## *Our Josh is Gone*

The walk back to the waiting room to tell our family and friends that Josh is gone was like walking through cement. It was only 8:30 a.m. but I felt as if we had endured a full day already. Johnny, Macy and I held hands as we walked in silence. The doors open and I see all those who are closest to us standing there. They are on pins and needles, waiting for any news.

"Josh died at 8:06 a.m. and is in Heaven now," I softly utter before breaking down in tears.

"He died," my mother asks in shock. "Oh my goodness, Laurie. He is gone?"

"Yes, Mama my baby is gone. My baby is gone!" I cry.

Sarah grabs me and hugs me tightly while our closest friends and family console Johnny and Macy. Everyone gathered in that waiting room -- family, friends, and USC Upstate personnel-- are crying.

I repeat over and over, "We have lost our Josh to a tragic accident. My precious baby boy has been taken from us. Why? Why Lord, why my baby."

I don't receive an answer from God or anyone in the room. No one utters a word yet all we can feel is love from our family and dearest friends.

My family wants to go see Josh and tell him goodbye. But they have to wait because the investigators from the Coroner's Office are at Josh's bedside now. Needing to sit down, I go back to the blasted consult room again. Johnny's mom, his aunt Nancy, Lisa's friend Janet, and Nick Crocker all try to console me but I feel sick and have to escape the room again. I remain in disbelief.

I work in this very hospital and my next shift will begin in less than 24 hours. I have to contact the doctors and my co-workers, those I work with for 10 hours a day, four/five days a week. Dr. M. Ryan Laye gives me his deepest condolences and kindly offers to contact everyone in the office for me. Before we hang up, he tells me to take as much time as I need. It takes me a few minutes to regain my composure before I can call Debbie Peevler. I know I will lose it as soon as she says hello. I tell Debbie about the car accident and that Josh has been killed along with three of his friends and one who survived but don't know her condition.

Debbie says, "Laurie I am so sorry!"

We both are crying and I can't form the words to tell her what has just happened to our Josh. I can only tell her I will call her when I know about the arrangements.

"I will be praying for all of you," Debbie tells me.

"Debbie, we need all the prayers we can to get through this nightmare," I tell her as I hang up and return to the waiting room where I sit with my sisters and mom.

I notice the silence. The whole ICU waiting room is quiet.

I look around and everyone's head is bowed. Family, friends, USC Upstate personnel, Sam, Mr. White, and total strangers all sit with heads bowed as if they are in church. They keep their heads bowed as they try to accept that our Josh has just taken away from us. The silence is broken with sobs and sniffles. My heart racing, I want Johnny. I need Johnny.

I find him in the consult room where the doctors informed us our Josh was going to die. We sit together looking downward deep in thought. Macy is with us. All three of us sit in the room that I despise with images of our Josh running rampant through our minds. Images of Sam pulling Josh from the burning car. Images of Josh lying lifeless as the machines work diligently to pump the air, blood, and medications into his broken body. Images of Josh bleeding, hurt and fighting to live. Images of Josh taking his last breath. The images stop only when we ask ourselves if we have made the right decision to discontinue life support and not do CPR.

"Really! Is this really happening? Really," I scream to myself and I tell Johnny and Macy that I have got to see my baby again. We have to see our Josh.

"This can't be the last time I see and hold my baby. God why? Why did you take Josh? Why him Lord? Why?"

It was around 10:00 a.m. when the coroner enters the consult room and asks everyone but immediate family to leave the room. The coroner and his investigators take seats and the coroner begins explaining that Josh died from massive chest and brain trauma. It will be up the pathologist to determine if and when an autopsy will be warranted but the coroner doubts it will be necessary.

"The toxicology levels will be sent to the South Carolina Law Enforcement Division, as standard of care, since Josh and the others are fatalities in a motor vehicle accident. Speed was an obvious factor in the accident," Coroner Rusty Clevenger explains softly and tells us the results will take at least 6-8 weeks.

"Will James's toxicology level be released to us," I ask. James was the driver and although Johnny and I had never met him, we have to know the truth.

"I have to notify James' parents first but then I will let you know," Rusty tells us. "This is a high profile case now. Four student athletes from USC Upstate have perished in a tragic accident. The media will be all over this."

The coroner and his investigators give all their condolences; hug us and especially Macy since she worked as an investigator at the coroner's office before. He also gives us permission to see Josh one more time.

The nurses escort the three of us to Josh's room where he is lying on his back and seems to be sleeping. But, my heart knows otherwise. The nurses have cleaned up Josh and tried to make him more presentable. Josh is now wearing a hospital gown with the sheet pulled up to his chest. His arms rest naturally beside his body. I hold his beautiful face in my hands, kissing every inch of it and begging God to please take care of my baby. I gently rub his forehead and run my hand through his blond hair. I tenderly touch his skin so I can remember the softness and texture of it. I feel his precious nose and his perfectly formed lips. I hold his hand and rub his crooked pinky finger on his left hand. I place my hand over his lifeless heart wishing the whole time to wake from this terrible nightmare. Unfortunately, this is not a nightmare. This is real. My Josh, Our Josh, has gone to Heaven.

Johnny and Macy say their goodbyes, telling Josh how much they love him while crying tears of sorrow. Johnny and I just stand there, each of us holding a hand of our beloved son. Tears stream down our faces as the anguish and heartbreak of losing our son becomes a reality.

I kiss by baby boy goodbye and tell him, "Wait on me son. Wait on us. We love you baby!"

I feel my heart break into pieces as I leave my baby at the hospital. My mind is telling me that Josh's soul and spirit are in a better place but, my heart is ripping into a thousand pieces; shattering all over the floor.

The three of us return to the waiting room to tell our family what the coroner revealed to us. Like us, they sit there in total disbelief that Josh is now gone. We are now in the midst of the nightmare that every parent has had and wishes they never have to endure. Our Josh, who loved everyone he met and who was loved back for having taken them into his life, has been taken from our lives. He has been stricken off the face of this Earth. Four USC Upstate athletes, who were all beautiful and strong, are gone in a split second on 4th Street in Boiling Springs, South Carolina.

We say our goodbyes to everyone in the Trauma/Surgical waiting room and know that they will soon be at our house. My feet won't allow me to leave. I can't leave my son. I can't leave my Josh, our Josh's body at the hospital. We left the unit in complete silence. We all walk back down the cream colored desolate halls back to the emergency room entrance to go home.

Steve offers to drive us home and we eventually follow him in complete silence. We all get in Johnny's truck and no one speaks a word. Again, the silence is only pierced with sobs and sniffles.

## HEAVEN CAN'T WAIT

Please don't go, stay awhile and talk?
But Mama, Heaven can't wait.
Let's go grab a bite to eat?
But Mama, Heaven can't wait.
Let's go take a long drive in your black truck?
But Mama, Heaven can't wait.
Let's watch a movie?
But, Mama, Heaven can't wait.
Let's go take a walk?
But mama, Heaven can't wait.
Why did you have to go so soon?
Because Mama, Heaven couldn't wait.

# THE EARTH STANDS STILL

The day you left us the Earth stood still.
My eyes were open but I couldn't see.
My ears were listening but I couldn't hear.
For our hearts were broken that only time will heal.
The day you left us the Earth stood still.
You left us without saying goodbye.
You left us pleading with God for a miracle.
For we had to let you go to be taken home where you belonged.
The day you left us the Earth stood still.
We couldn't feel the breeze blowing.
We couldn't feel the chill in the air.
For all we could do was cry tears of sorrow that showed our
deepest love.
The day you left us the Earth stood still.
We will no longer get to hold you tight.
We will no longer be able to say good night.
For all we can do is say our prayers and thank the Good Lord for
your amazing grace.
The day you left us the Earth stood still.
You just wait on us up in Heaven above.
You just laugh and sing in perfect harmony.
For it's all in Gods good time that we will be together again.
For now the Earth stands still.

# CHAPTER FIVE
## *The Media Coverage*

Steve turns into our driveway where several vehicles are parked. I don't recognize any of the cars. I step out of the truck and immediately spot my cousin Larry Floyd, who my immediate family calls Scooter. Scooter grabs me and I cry as he hugs and hugs me. He explains what Johnny and I should expect to going through during the next couple of days. Scooter and his wife Gina lost their baby girl Katie to cancer when she was just a toddler. He tells me not to forget Johnny and Macy. Scooter wants me to be aware and reminded that they too will be grieving and hurting just as much as I am.

"Hold each other tight, Laurie."

Sean and Keath are standing outside my home and they hug all of us while giving their condolences.

"If there is anything we need please, do not hesitate to ask."

I stand still listening to Johnny talk with Sean Henderson and Keath Roberts. Looking down, I realize that I am wearing green. I shake my head thinking it is only fitting for me to have on green, which are the USC Upstate colors….the University that my Josh fell in love with the moment he walked onto that campus. This wasn't a coincidence. The Lord called upon me to grab that green shirt. He knew!

I walk into the house to see Michelle Henderson and Shannon Roberts tidying up and they both hug me. They begin crying, too. There are no words to express the pain radiating between us and the grief that is taking over our lives.

Then I see it. My baby's blood is all over me.

These bloodstains represent Josh's life. Josh's life was taken from him and from us in an avoidable manner. I begin crying again. I can't get the image of my baby lying in that ICU unit injured and fighting for his life. I tell Michelle and Shannon that I need a shower and thank them for straightening up. Both assured me not to worry about it.

I step into the shower and I just stand there letting the warm water cascade over me. The tears begin to flow again and I weep. I cry like I have never have cried before. I even hear myself wail as my mind races. The images are replaying in my mind. Johnny, Macy and I pray and plead to God not to take our Josh.

"Please, God! Make these images stop. Please make them stop," I whisper as the warm water continues to run over me. "Please take these images of Josh being so hurt. Please forever erase them from my thoughts.

Many images of Josh ricochet through my mind. All of our dreams for Josh have been destroyed.

Johnny and I get dressed and the realization that we are going have to bury our child begins sinking in. Our nightmare is just beginning. We cling to each other for strength.

My sisters, Lisa and Macy, keep telling me not to get on Facebook or watch the news. But, as Josh's mom, I want to know what happened. Johnny and I both have the right to know what happened to our baby.

I sit down in the recliner and just stare at my cellphone. Do I pick it up and look at Facebook? Macy notices my expression and reads my mind. "Mama, Facebook has pictures of the car. Mama, you don't need to look at that right now." She takes my phone and puts it in the bedroom on my nightstand.

Johnny is outside with all his friends and I am indoors with my mom and sisters. Macy and Lisa go outside to meet their friends who have just arrived. Brian and Teresa Dailey and their daughter Kaylyn arrive and they give us their heartfelt condolences, too. Macy's boyfriend Michael Chadwick arrives and goes straight to Johnny. Haila Adams and her daughter Jade stop by and I tell Haila what I know about the accident. "How in the world am I going to be able to work knowing I can see the room Josh died in day in and day out," I cry.

In her calm manner, Haila tells me, "Laurie, every time you look to the left you can say that you were there when Jesus and His angels came to get Josh. How remarkable it is to know that you were in the presence of Jesus."

Haila is exactly right! A transcending calm comes over me as I realize that Johnny, Macy, and I were in the same room when Jesus came to get my baby. I can say that we were there when Josh came into this world and we were there when Jesus and his angels took Josh to Heaven. Not everyone can witness this indescribable experience. We go silent again as we each recount all that has happened in the last eight hours.

Our house soon fills with family and friends. All I want to do is go hide in my bedroom. Pulling the covers over me will allow me to escape reality. I don't want to face what was ahead of me. I can't face what is ahead of me. Maybe if I pretend that this was just a dream maybe it wasn't real. But, I can't. I am Josh's mom. I have to represent him and face reality. My number one priority is to learn what happened to my Josh, our Josh.

My brief retreat ends with Lisa running into the house, "The media is here and they want an interview."

Anger fills my body. I am mad at the world. I am angry at Josh for getting in that car. I am angry at God. I am angry at James for driving recklessly, angry at Johnny for letting Josh live on campus, and I am angry at myself for constantly fussing at Josh for having a dirty room.

I' m so angry that I decide to march outside and have my say about losing my son. Josh was taken from me and I am angry. As I head toward the news team, a calming presence falls over me again; a shield of peace maybe. All the anger and hurt leave me. I become proud and honored to speak about my son. Johnny meets the media before I can get there. They stand in the driveway and I march right up to them. Nothing or no one is going to prevent me from telling the world about my Josh, our beloved Josh.

The female reporter begins asking questions. "How are you feeling right now?"

Johnny and I both respond, "We are in shock. Our pain right now is indescribable."

"Tell me about Josh."

"If you knew Josh, you knew love. If you knew my son, you knew laughter. Josh loved his family with all his heart and he treasured his teammates as family," I tell her, the words just coming to me in the midst of grieving. "Josh loved and showered everyone he met with his love for mankind and brought laughter into a depressed world. There wasn't a day that went by that Josh never smiled or laughed. EVER!"

Johnny picks up when I can no longer speak, "Josh was a

true Spartan. Josh fell in love with USC Upstate the moment he walked onto that campus."

The reporter and the cameraman give us their condolences and thank us for the interview. Johnny and I say our goodbyes and head back inside. I am crying inconsolably again and Lisa leads me into the house. Macy remains outside with her friends Jessica, Brandy, and Ridge. I am glad Macy's friends are with her. She needs them.

As the day goes on, more and more of our friends and family come to our house. Our front yard is full of cars. It is close to 3 p.m. when Courtney and her mom finally arrive. Courtney has the sweetest personality. She is just like our Josh. She is always smiling or giggling. Josh and Courtney were a match made in heaven.

"I am so sorry Courtney, so sorry. I tried to keep Josh alive. I tried," I tell her as we both sob and hold each other tight.

"It's ok. It's ok," she whispers.

Johnny walks up and hugs Courtney and then takes her off to the side.

Amy, Courtney's mom, stays with me and I ask, "How is she doing?"

"She is okay. Courtney is okay," Amy tells me and then asks how we are doing.

I tell her what I know about the accident and what happened at the hospital.

Some of Josh's teammates and classmates are now in the house with Coach Smith and Coach Blackwelder who all hug us and give us their heartfelt condolences. Several of the young men are crying and looking into their eyes I see how heartbroken they are at the loss of their friend and teammate. I find myself comforting them.

People have brought so much food to our house that we send some of it home with Josh's teammates and for Courtney to share with Josh's roommates Sam and Rinaldi. The coaches, teammates, classmates and especially Courtney all hug us goodbye and give Johnny, Macy and myself their condolences before returning to the university.

USC Upstate brings in counselors to talk about the loss of four teammates and classmates but, especially their friends who died today. The coaches are meeting with each individual sport to talk about their loss and grief. They share memories of Josh, Mills, Sarah and James with each other. This gives them time to reminisce about the four friends lost in a tragic accident. They cry, comfort each other, mourn, and try to make sense of the accident.

Night has fallen when Johnny and I sit down to watch the news. The car accident is the lead news and it's the first time I see the car. The white, 2014 Mustang convertible is wrapped around the tree on 4th Street. The car is split in half with the front wheels hugging one another. Smoke surrounds the car.

Nausea overcomes me as I think about those precious babies perishing in that crumpled, mangled car. Horrific images rush at me of Josh, James, Mills and Sarah and of Felicia, the lone survivor.

The questions come at me just as fast. Did they suffer? Did James, Mills and Sarah die on impact? How is Felicia? Has her family made it to her bedside yet? Did Sam and the other two good Samaritans get hurt trying to save all those babies? Did they see them perishing in the fire? Did Josh try to talk when Sam and the other two Samaritans got him out? Was my baby scared and hurting? How long did it take to get Josh to the hospital? I want answers to why my Josh, our Josh was taken from us.

Johnny and I sit in our living room watching the news. We are stunned and unable to move as we watch our tragedy unfold on our television. Josh's picture is plastered on the screen as reporters remark that the Spartanburg County Coroner has identified the victims. The VICTIMS! That is all I hear. My baby! My Josh is a victim; forever a statistic in the books of motor vehicle accidents. Every news channel is reporting the accident and about Josh. We are constantly seeing and hearing about the victims. The reporters name each one by one, except Mills who has yet to be identified by the coroner. The media personalizes the news by telling each name, where they are from and what sport they played. They also mention that toxicology reports are pending.

My heart breaks over and over again each time I see Josh's picture on the television screen. A gut wrenching pain fills in my abdomen as if a knife is twisting into my soul. These feelings and torturous images are tearing me apart. I just want to wake up from this nightmare. I want to run to Josh's apartment to confirm this is only a dream. But, in reality it isn't. My baby has been taken from me. I will never be the same person. October 11, 2015 at 8:06 a.m. has forever altered my life. That morning has forever changed Johnny, Macy and me.

# REALITY

My son is gone
Never coming back, ever.
My heart bleeds from the pain of my loss of losing my child.
Moments in time has stopped.
I'm lost, confused, mad, sad, and just plain angry.
Angry with Josh for getting in that blasted car.
Angry at God for taking my son.
Angry at the driver for his unjustified actions.
Really!
Really is this happening?
Really never seeing him again.
Really never touching his face or seeing his smile or hearing him laugh.
Really!
Really!
How do you move on?
How do you get over this?
How do we move on knowing my son is gone?
Died the word is taboo but my son died.
He is gone to never return home.
Why?
Why?
What is the reason?
I have to know the reason.
Really!
Reality is for real.

# CHAPTER SIX
## *The SC Highway Patrol Visit*

y sisters, my mom, and Lisa are still at my house when the doorbell rings. I answer the door and there stands two South Carolina Highway Patrol officers. Panic overcomes me again. They introduce themselves and ask if they can speak to Joshua Lee's parents. Johnny and Macy are immediately at my side and the three of us step outside to speak with the officers in private. Macy knows both officers from working with the coroner's office. They embrace her tightly and keep saying, "We are so sorry, Macy. So, so sorry for yall's loss."

Macy thanks them and they immediately turn their attention to Johnny and me. Johnny shakes their hands and introduces us. Both patrolmen nodded and tipped their hats in my direction.

"On behalf of the South Carolina Highway Patrol, we want to extend our deepest condolences on the loss of your son, Josh."

Through our tears, Johnny and I thank them as they hand me a victims advocate booklet that details a progression of events of what to expect and tips on how to handle the upcoming planning of Josh's funeral. The booklet has much needed information and phone numbers about how to recover the police report (MAIT) but mostly how to handle OUR grief. Later that night I read every single word of the booklet. Needless to say I cried but it did help me understand what to expect in the next few days.

We ask the patrolmen if they have determined exactly what happened and cause of the accident. Up to this point all Johnny and I know is what we have heard from the various news reports. The lead patrolman explains that after questioning the witnesses this is all they have to go on until the MAIT report will be conducted and reviewed.

"What is a MAIT report," I ask.

"A MAIT report is an official investigation where the Highway Patrol will reconstruct the accident and determine the speed and cause, if a cause, can be determined. The report can take up to six to eight weeks to get it back," the patrolman explains.

"Will a toxicology report be done on the driver," I ask.

They both nod and explain, "No ma'am. Because the driver died at the scene no one will be charged. We will not be conducting a toxicology screen on the driver. But, it will be done by the Spartanburg County Coroner's office."

The lead patrolman says, "Speed was an obvious factor because of the destructive damage that the vehicle sustained from the impact. We estimated the car was going at least 70-80 mph on impact. No brakes were applied that we could tell at the time but the car also caught fire on impact. After questioning the witnesses it was determined that the survivor was able to get out of the car on her own accord and Mr. Cheshier was first upon the scene. The other two gentlemen's last names are Burnett and Richard. Mr. Cheshier was trying to get Josh out when the other two came upon the scene. Mr. Cheshier was screaming, "Help me get them out! Help me get them out!" Sam and the other two got Josh out and laid him upon the pavement away from the car and Sam told Josh he would be right back. Josh was breathing."

The officers tell us that Sam and the other two men tried to get the front seat passenger out but couldn't. They went around to the driver but, he was trapped by the motor. By this time the car was fully engulfed by the fire and they went back to Josh's side waiting on the ambulance to arrive.

We would learn days later that Sam held Josh, telling him "Hang on buddy. Hang on, Josh, they're on their way."

To know that Josh was being comforted by his best friend makes me feel better but, I should have been the one to comfort him. I should have been the one to hold my son and tell him to hang on. As Josh's mother, it should have been me to rub his head and wipe away the blood and tears.

Johnny, Macy and I stand on the front porch in complete silence with the officers. Johnny speaks first and thanks them both for coming. The officers assured us if we need anything to please call them. I was teary and really couldn't speak. All I could do was just stand there, gasping for air because of the images in my mind of my baby hurting and bleeding and needing his Mama. I wasn't there to help my baby and protect him.

"Why? Why Lord? Why," is all I can think and ask?

The three of us wave goodbye to the officers and go back inside. Johnny and I are exhausted, mentally and physically. Lisa wants to stay with us. Macy escapes to her bedroom and Johnny and I to ours. We wearily crawl into bed where we hug one another and cry for our son. No words are needed between us. We both know that each other's hearts are broken. We toss and turn all night. Our bodies are heavy with exhaustion but our minds will not shut down for the much needed rest.

I lie in the dark bedroom and strain to hear Josh or feel his presence near me. My daddy died 10 years ago and I remember being half asleep when he called my name, awakening me with a jolt. I want Josh to call my name so desperately. At one time during the night I feel heaviness upon my legs and the bed seems to shift. I call out "Josh," then the weight lifts. Maybe Josh did come to us to let me know he is okay. I am a strong believer that God does send your loved ones back or sends signs that they are okay. We just have to be quiet and look and listen for God to speak to us.

## LOOKING DOWN FROM HEAVEN

As I sit in Heaven and look down upon you I see sadness and
tears all because of me. I am one of God's favorite Angels so
please don't cry.

I am with you in spirit of every minute of every day. Just look for
my signs that I haven't really went away.

You can feel my embrace as you close your eyes and see my face.
I am always near just call my name and I will be there.

The Lord has given me a set of the most beautiful wings. I have
the ability to fly and sit atop of a star.

It's an amazing sight I wish you could see.

I can slide down rainbows and soar above the mountain tops. It's
as magical as I hold you within my heart.

I am looking down and hear you wishing for answers. It is all in
God's good time before we all can be together again. Be patient, for
God will deliver those answers in due time.

Until that day comes just try to smile and laugh with joy.

For I am smiling down upon you all. I will forever be with you
embedded in your memories.

I am always looking down from Heaven.

## THE BLACK CHEVY TRUCK

There is a black Chevy truck that remains parked in silence.
For the truck had to say good bye to its owner.
The truck holds all the memories of traveling with you on
South Carolina highways.
It took you to all your favorite places.
For the truck holds all your secrets, your dreams, but mostly
your precious memories.
For the truck heard your laughter, your tears of sorrow, your
conversations and your ability to break into a joyous song.
The black truck took you on your first date and it took you on
your last. For its motor was as powerful as you.
But for now the truck's engine will remain silent. For the Black
Chevy mourns its driver. Forever remaining parked.

# CHAPTER SEVEN
## *Planning Josh's Funeral*

J ohnny and I are showered and dressed by 6 a.m. on
Monday, October 12, 2015. We go downstairs to find
Lisa up too. We let Macy sleep in so she can get some
rest. The house is quiet. Johnny turns on the television and it
all comes rushing back! The news is still reporting the accident
and every 15 minutes Josh's photo appears on the screen. His
beautiful smile and his baby blue eyes are staring at us. Johnny
and I just sit there staring at the television. We are so choked up
that neither of us can speak. Needing to flee the media reports,
I go outside and sit in a rocking chair. The rocking chair and
porch become my escape. It is so peaceful out here and there is
a cool, crisp breeze.

I look to the beautiful blue sky and pray for God to answer
me. "Why? Lord, why?"

I pray for strength to get us through the day.

"One day at a time is what I ask from you," I say to God.

Sitting there I watch a group of birds take flight and I listen to them sing their joyous sounds. Even in this serene setting, my mind reflects back to Josh being so badly injured. The images replay in my mind over and over.

"Did we make the right decision to disconnect all means of life support and not do CPR?" I continue my conversation with God. "I have heard of miracles where people come back when the doctors say they are brain dead. Maybe we didn't fight hard enough for Josh. But, Josh was so broken from his chest injuries. This is just not happening. Not to our Josh."

While I am outside talking to God, Johnny receives a call from Dunbar Funeral Home to tell us what time to come to Floyd's Greenlawn Cemetery. We are to pick out Josh's grave, make arrangements for Josh's celebration of life ceremony, and pick out a casket. A casket? We should not be picking out a casket for our child. This is just not the right sequence of events of living. A child buries a parent. A parent does not bury their child. Every parent's worst nightmare has become a reality. The unimaginable is really happening to us.

Our family arrives again as we are leaving to plan Josh's funeral.

"Please tell anyone who comes to the house why Johnny and I aren't here to greet them," I tell my family.

As we leave the house, Johnny's cell phone rings. It is Tammy Whaley.

"USC Upstate is holding a candlelight vigil tonight for Josh, James, Mills and Sarah. Do you and your family want to attend," she asks.

"Absolutely," Johnny tells her with no hesitation. "Can USC Upstate provide us with a Spartan flag to drape over Josh's casket? I think he will like that better than flowers. Can you also arrange for us to bury him in USC Upstate apparel?"

"Let me work on it and I will bring everything to your house in a little while. I also want to interview you and Laurie for a media story and our website," says Tammy.

"We will do anything for you and USC Upstate," Johnny tells Tammy as he becomes teary. "Josh loved that college and the college life so much. He wanted to experience college life to the fullest and he accomplished that goal even though it was cut way too short."

I am nervous as we drive to the cemetery and my tears begin to flow again as we pull into the parking lot. Johnny and I should not have to select a grave plot and plan a funeral for our child. No parent should have to endure this horror. No parent should ever have to go through this nightmare. I want answers!

Johnny and I make our way to the door when I notice two cardinals sitting in the tree adjacent to the building. They are in plain sight. I have never seen such vibrant red birds before and now there are two here for me to see before I pick out my son's grave. Before she died, my grandmother always told me that when you see a red bird it means a loved one has come down from Heaven to check on you. I actually smile. I knew in my heart that these two cardinals are Josh and my Daddy. They are here with us to let me know Josh is okay. This may all sound crazy but, I'll say it again, I believe God does show signs that our loved ones are with Him.

I am smiling as we sit in the lobby to wait for a funeral representative. He takes us back to his office and begins to review the paper work including the cost of the plot and different areas in the cemetery where we can choose Josh's resting place. Johnny handles the details and the financial arrangements while I look around at the numerous grave markers. There are so many different designs. They range from small ones, large ones, single and multi-family ones. You can have a color pictorials placed on the marker with different quotes. The markers can be black, silver, bronze and even gold.

I am overwhelmed will all there is to choose from but I know Josh's marker is going to be simple. After all, Josh was a simple person who didn't want or care for luxury items.

"The simpler the better," is what Josh would always say.

But, we did want "Just Chillin" on his marker. Any time we asked Josh, "What are you doing?" He would always respond "Just Chillin!"

I also want Josh's picture in his USC Upstate travel sweat suit on his marker. It just seems appropriate.

Johnny gets my attention and we follow the funeral worker to his personal SUV. As we exit the building, I look up in the tree trying to catch a glimpse of the two cardinals. But, they have already flown off. The man drives us around to the very back portion of the cemetery where I spot a garden.

"This is the perfect place for Josh," I say.

Every plot in this area has already been taken so we look at several more options. One is in the middle of the area and I just walk around. I don't want to do this. How are we to decide where to place our child for his everlasting resting place? This is not right and not normal.

We drive to another part of the cemetery where some plots are available near the drive and wooded area. Johnny stands where Josh will be laid and just stares towards the east. Johnny is rocking up and down on his feet and I can tell that picking out his son's grave is absolutely killing him. My heart aches for Johnny who has tears forming in his eyes.

"This is the plot we want for our Josh," says Johnny. "Are there available plots beside Josh?"

"Yes, but you do not have to buy them now. But, I highly recommend you to do so in the near future to avoid strangers buying them and trying to resale them to you for double or triple the price."

"Excuse me? What did you say," I ask, feeling my anger begin to build.

"Josh is a young adult and he is considered a high profile individual. Total strangers will buy plots beside him in an effort to make money off you. They know you will pay any amount to have your everlasting resting place beside your son," he tells us as if this was common knowledge.

I was stunned. Seriously? How wrong and evil this world has become for someone to buy a burial plot just because they know a grieving parent will pay any amount to be beside their loved ones, especially their child? There is a place in this universe for people who do this and it is called Hell! Literally!

Johnny immediately places a hold on the adjoining plots and says that we will purchase them soon. We return to the office and I again look for the cardinals. There is no sign of them.

As we drive back home, all I can think about is Josh being alone in that grave with nobody he knows near him.

"Please God, take care of my baby. Just please take care of my baby," I pray.

As we pull into the driveway, I see that more of our family has arrived and Macy is sitting on the front porch.

"Are you okay, baby girl?" I ask her tenderly.

"Yeah, I'm okay," she says as we enter the house.

My mom and sisters greet us and tell us someone delivered chicken biscuits. Johnny and I try to eat but simply cannot.

An hour later Tammy Whaley is here to interview us and she has a bag of USC Upstate clothing for us to consider burying Josh in. Johnny chooses a grey Spartan t-shirt and a long sleeve knit, athletic warm-up jacket with the Spartan emblem on the left chest area. I already have his khaki pants ready. My sister Tammy bought Josh black Nike crew socks since we cannot go to his apartment yet to get his belongings.

Josh always wore black crew socks. It didn't matter what he

was wearing. Josh only wore black crew socks. I would tease him, "Older men are the ones that wear black socks." Josh would just respond with, "Yeah, yeah, Laurie Anne." Then we would both laugh.

Johnny, Macy and I sit with down with Tammy for the interview. She asks us about Josh and his family.

"If you knew Josh, you knew love. If you knew my son, you knew laughter. Josh loved his family with all his heart and he treasured his teammates as family," I tell her. "Josh loved everyone, everyone. He never saw the color of skin or social class."

Johnny adds, "Josh was a true Spartan."

Macy speaks up and says, "My brother was my better half. He was the peanut butter to my jelly. He has grown into a very special young man and he made us so proud. I will cherish the memories I had with him forever."

I begin to sob. Macy has lost her brother. My family unit is broken.

I hold Macy's hand and rest my head upon hers. Johnny sits quietly, wringing his hands. We tell Tammy about Josh's surviving family members and thank her again. She tells us what time to be on campus for the candlelight vigil and asks me my maiden name.

"Floyd," I tell her trying to figure out why she asks.

"We will reserve parking spaces for your family under your maiden name. There will be lots of media there and I don't want them to approach you as you try to enter the soccer stadium," Tammy explains.

"They will literally stop us and try to interview us?" I ask.

Tammy replies, "Yes. I am sorry."

She lets a few seconds pass before asking us, "Are y'all okay with being in the same room as the other parents?"

"Absolutely," Johnny and I reply in unison.

"What happened to our babies is not the other parents'

fault. We all have lost our babies in an awful accident. We were able to touch Josh, kiss and tell him goodbye. But the other parents didn't get that chance. If Josh had perished like Mills, James and Sarah, I would need proof that Josh was in that coffin," I tell her and Johnny agrees.

Tammy hugs us with tears in her eyes as she leaves our house. The three of us get ready to go to the funeral home where we will pick out Josh's casket and plan his Celebration of Life Ceremony. I instruct my mom and sister to tell anyone who comes to the house where we are, thank them for coming, and we are sorry we missed them. They assure me they will handle it.

"What song did Josh and his friends like to listen to?" I ask Macy once we are in the car.

"The *Fast and the Furious* Song," she tells me as she finds it for me to listen.

The song is beautiful and perfect; even though I only hear the first two stanzas. It has a sweet melody to it.

I squeeze Johnny's hand every few seconds as he drives us to the funeral home. He knows that I am nervous and sick to my stomach knowing that we are going to pick out a casket for our baby.

"How does a parent choose a casket for their child," I ask again. "There isn't one made perfectly enough for our Josh! Period!"

At the funeral home, Mr. Dunbar's secretary greets us and escorts us into a conference room. She offers us water or coffee but we all decline.

"Mr. Dunbar will be with you shortly," she says.

"Thank you," Johnny tells her.

As we wait on Mr. Dunbar, my mind begins firing off questions. Is my baby here yet? Will they let me see him? Just how bad is he? Does he look like my Josh? The questions don't stop so I say under by breath, "You can do this. Do this for Josh. Be strong, Laurie. God, please let us get through this."

Mr. Dunbar shakes hands and speaks with Johnny first. He turns his attention to me offering his deepest condolences. We sit down and he tells us that Josh is here and he will take good care of him. Johnny and I both thank him.

"My son was two years old when he died in a drowning accident. He will always be my child. We still have his room. Josh will forever be your child and you should address him that way," Mr. Dunbar tells us.

I am crying again and Johnny just nods his head.

Yes, Josh will be forever our child, our Josh.

"Do you have a lawyer?" Mr. Dunbar asks.

"No, should we?" Johnny answers.

Mr. Dunbar shares with us that his teenage son Mac was hit by a drunk driver while walking to class at the University of South Carolina. Mac was critically injured and required several surgeries and intensive rehabilitation.

"We have been fighting with insurance companies for a while now so I highly recommend contacting your lawyer and your own personal car insurance carrier as soon as possible," Mr. Dunbar advises.

Johnny assures him that we will do so by the end of the week. This advice would prove to help us more than anyone could have ever imagined. The thought of having to fight and battle insurance companies to pay bills for a cut and dry case just unnerves me. This is a whole other story in itself. Literally!

Mr. Dunbar asks us what we want in specifics of Josh's funeral. I tell him the four songs I want sung and pictures I want displayed throughout the ceremony.

He asks, "What are the songs so I can listen to them?"

I begin explaining, "Amazing Grace is Josh's favorite gospel song and he would randomly burst out singing it no matter where he was and he would sing it to everyone. The Lord's Prayer because I believe this song praises God and it needs to be included in the service. The third song is When I Get Where I'm Going by Brad Paisley and Dolly Parton because I know where Josh is going and I know in my heart and soul that Josh is being greeted by our Lord Jesus Christ and my Daddy. After Jesus sees Josh I hope my Daddy gets ahold of him real good. Fussing at him for getting in that blasted car. The last song is "See You Again", from *The Fast and Furious 7* soundtrack. It is by Wiz Khalifa and features Charlie Puth. This song represents the bonds that Josh and his teammates, classmates, friends, and family held that will never be broken. Also, we will see each other again.

We want Josh's body be brought out of the sanctuary with this song and all the USC Upstate athletes to follow him. All USC Upstate athletes are to be honorary pallbearers.

Dr. Dunbar offers to arrange for a singer and a pianist and we thankfully agree.

"Do you want to have visitation at the funeral home or your house," Mr. Dunbar asks. "Have you decided on an open or a closed casket? You can have an open casket but, everyone will try in earnest to see Josh's injuries."

My heart can't stand the thought of people staring at my baby. We want people to remember our Josh; our handsome, beautiful son who smiled and laughed every day.

Johnny, Macy and I decide to have visitation at our house. Our family will be more comfortable at the house instead of standing in a receiving line for hours and hours. We also decide on a closed casket.

Those decisions made, Mr. Dunbar escorts us to pick out Josh's casket and vault. I immediately become nervous and my stomach is twisting into knots; double knots matter of fact. We follow him into a room full of half caskets and vaults. I am overwhelmed with the choices of color, bedding, and decorative item. I wonder around the room crying the whole time and I keep repeating, "This is not happening. This is not happening."

Johnny and Macy are standing beside a mahogany colored casket with cream bedding. The casket has porcelain angels on each corner. I look at Johnny and nod my head. Johnny knows too, this is the one. Because, Josh is now and will forever be our angel. Josh will be everyone's guardian angel.

"You can choose an angel or cross to be mounted on each corner," says Mr. Dunbar.

Johnny and I say simultaneously, "Angel."

Mr. Dunbar tells us that each angel will be taken off and made into a memorial setting for us to keep. I began gently rubbing the angel and pleading with God again, "Take care of my baby, please."

We leave the mortuary in silence, again. I want to go back and be with Josh. He was all alone. In my mind I know his soul and spirit is in Heaven. But, my heart wants him back here with us.

Josh was needed here laughing, smiling, and aggravating me. Saying to me, "Laurie Anne, seriously!"

All these images of my baby lying in a mortuary all alone are killing me. I feel like I can't breathe. I need air. I normally handle situations involving undue circumstances well but, this is ripping me apart. A part of my heart and soul are now lying in Dunbar's Mortuary. My baby boy has died. He is never coming back home. EVER!

## "WE WILL"

We will see you again one day.
We will see those sparkling baby blues.
We will see that contagious smile.
We will feel your face and touch your hair too.
We will feel your embrace.
We will sing high on that mountain Amazing Grace.
We will laugh and we will cry.
We will ride the shooting stars with you in the sky.
We will sit and talk with the man in moon.
We will dance from dusk to noon.
We will sit together and pray.
We will see you again one day.

## THE LITTLE WOODEN CROSS

There is a little wooden cross that was given to me the day
you died.
Since that day the cross hasn't left my side.
I grasped that little wooden cross with all my might.
At that single moment I knew everything was going to be alright.
That little wooden cross had the strength that can only come
from above.
For it's a symbol of the purest of true love.
With that little wooden cross I began praying to God to explain
to us why?
That little wooden cross never answered but I knew this wasn't
our final goodbyes.
For that little wooden cross saved my life that day.
For I knew then that you were in Heaven and that little wooden
cross was our only passageway.
For I will always hold that little wooden cross close to my heart.
For God knew you were His angel from the start.

# CHAPTER EIGHT
## The Little Wooden Cross

We arrive back home to find Sean and Mike Wilson cutting our grass. We will be forever grateful to them for that act of kindness. I notice the yard is full of vehicles but only recognize the cars of my immediate family. Our house is full of people. Some of the faces I know but, mostly they are Johnny's customers from the station.

Johnny and I decide which picture of Josh we want enlarged to have on display by his casket at his funeral. We chose the one with Josh in a white sports coat and turquoise shirt and tie. His contagious smile was beaming in it, too. His baby blues catch your attention and are pronounced because of the colors in his shirt. My sister Tammy takes the photo to Spartan Photo to have it enlarged for us. Spartan Photo donated three 16 x 20 portraits of Josh as their gift to Johnny and me. To see the enlarged portrait of Josh was just breathtaking. We are forever grateful to them to show such a wonderful act of kindness towards us.

The Spartanburg community loves Johnny for true honesty, kindness, and his work ethic. Most of Spartanburg County bring their cars to White's Pine Street Exxon and consider Johnny a friend. My heart is breaking but, at that moment I realize how much Johnny means to everyone. Since Josh worked for his Dad everyone knew him, too. They bring food, flowers, prayer blankets that have been prayed over, Bible verses, devotionals, and poems. But most importantly, they bring love and sympathy. Johnny introduces me to everyone and it is my honor to hug and express to them my deepest gratitude for showing us such kindness.

My sister April informs us that our preacher is here to go over the funeral. I grab Johnny and Macy and we head into the sitting room to discuss our plans with the preacher. Preacher Westafer asks us how we are doing and all we can say is "hanging in there. We are just hanging in there."

Preacher Westafer goes over details of the funeral and asks, "Do you anyone who is speaking on Josh's behalf?"

We know that Courtney wants to speak and I say, "I will be speaking, too."

Johnny, the preacher, and Macy just stare at me like I have just lost my mind. I was bound and determined to speak on my son's behalf. I knew exactly what I was going to say about my baby boy.

Earlier at the mortuary Mr. Dunbar told us he has witnessed parents trying to speak at their child's funeral and it usually doesn't end well. So, he didn't recommend that we attempt such a feat. Anyone who knows me knows that I am one determined and strong headed person. Once I set my mind on doing something, nothing, I mean nothing, can stop me. So, I am going to speak about my baby. I want people to know our Josh. Not the Josh they have heard about or seen on TV.

"Anyone else we know of," asks Preacher Westafer.

I look straight at Johnny and say, "Do you think Coach Skip Frye will talk about Josh for us?"

"I'm sure he will I will ask him when he gets here," Johnny says. "He called earlier and asked if he could come by and bring us ice and water."

We review the songs again and discuss which Bible verse was Josh favorite.

*Philippians 4:13*: "I can do all things through Christ which strengthened me," I tell them.

Preacher Westafer says the sweetest prayer over us before he leaves. He prays for comfort and for the Lord to help us mourn the loss of our Josh. I can feel the prayers being transformed into reality. The spirit of our Lord is with us. I just think I am pushing it away.

"How can a loving God take my child? Why my child? There were so many cruel and evil people and thugs in this world why did he have to take someone like my Josh, our Josh. A person who loved everyone and wanted to bring laughter and joy into everyone's lives he met. So, why my Josh, why take our Josh," I ask myself.

I didn't want to hear about God needing Josh for a reason or He needed another angel to help him. I need Josh. We need Josh. Maybe I was being selfish and wrong on questioning God's intentions. But, there is no other explanation anyone can give me during this time. Never!

Coach Frye arrives about an hour later. He was Josh's favorite teacher but mostly, Josh's favorite coach. Coach Frye was Josh's track and field coach. He inspired Josh and was a Godly man. Coach Frye has a way about him that makes the kids and anyone he meets love him. Maybe this is why Josh admired him so much. Coach Frye was not just a coach but, a friend to the athletes and to the kids he taught in school.

Johnny and I meet Coach Frye outside so we can talk in

private.

"Would you mind speaking for Josh at his funeral?" Johnny asks Coach Frye.

With tears in his eyes Coach Frye responds "It will be the greatest honor anyone has ever asked of me. It will be my pleasure."

We talk about the accident and how we had to remove Josh from life support. Coach Frye expresses his deepest condolences and tells us not to hesitate to ask him if we need anything.

Inside several of Josh's teachers, professors, and former principles are gathered to show their respect. The house is still full and my kitchen, dinette table, bar, and dining room, and both refrigerators inside and outside are full of food, drinks, eating utensils, paper goods, and bathroom tissue. I am overwhelmed and need to step outside to catch my breath. Being on my front porch has always given me peace and comfort. It is my refuge, my escape.

As I stepped onto the porch, I see my co-workers arriving. Everyone I work with is here. I know I will lose my composure just saying hello and I do. Working with my co-workers like mine, we all work as a family. So, this has hit home for everyone. I join them inside and we talk about the accident.

"I don't know how in the world I can work knowing every time look to the left I will see the room where Josh died," I tell them. "Haila told me yesterday that when I look to the left I can say that I was there when Jesus and His angels came and got Josh. How remarkable it is to know that we were in the presence of Jesus," I say and everyone is crying.

They all give me their prayers and condolences and say they will see us at the vigil as I head back outside. Debbie stays with me. She sits beside me and holds my hand. We rock in the rocking chairs and I tell her about my comfort place here on this porch. I tell her that we have visited the mortuary and we can open the casket but decided against it because of Josh's injuries.

"It will be okay," she says softly and we continue to rock.

I look up to see Johnny hugging a woman and they are crying. Johnny points in my direction and they start walking towards the porch. Johnny introduces her, "Laurie, this is Becky Dunbar, Jimmy Dunbar's wife."

I stand up and hug her for the longest time. I know she understands exactly the pain and turmoil I am experiencing this very moment. We both are crying and she asks me to please sit back down. Becky kneels beside me and Debbie stays at my side. As I explain to Becky that we can't open the casket because of Josh's injuries, she hands me a small wooden cross that fits perfectly in my palm.

"After my son died, I had one of these crosses and it helped me so much to keep my faith," she says as she hands me a devotional booklet. "When I would start to feel bad I would grab the cross and read a passage from the devotional. It raised my spirits and brought me closer to the Lord. I regained my faith for I knew that the Lord would help with the pain," she explains to me.

"Thank you," I say through my sobs as I grasp the little wooden cross in my hand.

Debbie hugs me goodbye as we both sit and cry on my front porch. No words are needed. I thank her for coming and thank her for everything she has done for me and will continue to do for me. After Debbie leaves, I just sit there and stare at my little wooden cross.

The longer I hold the little wooden cross the more power I feel from it. It is a feeling of an indescribable force being inserted into my heart and soul. It is a feeling of warmth and a feeling of strength. Mostly it is a feeling of love and courage. I realize that this little cross and the meaning behind it are my only passageway to see my baby boy again. I know in my heart that our Lord Jesus Christ will hold me tight and help us get through the loss our Josh. For I will always be grateful to Mrs. Dunbar for such a small but, powerful gift. That day on my front porch, a little wooden cross changes my life. It saves my life.

An hour after receiving the cross I feel Him near me and with us. I sit and hold my little cross. I pray to Him and ask Him to help me, help Johnny and Macy. Help us understand why He took Josh. I thought I was a Christian before the accident but, after receiving that cross and holding it enlightened my views of Christianity. Holding that cross for an hour and looking onto the horizon, I know that I am the one who has to speak for Josh. To finish Josh's race.

More friends and customers of Johnny's arrive to our house. Everyone is so nice and concerned about our well-being. Everyone gives us their heartfelt condolences and assures us that we are in their prayers. Johnny and I both are so grateful for the community of Spartanburg have come together over this tragedy. Johnny tells me that it was time to go the vigil that USC Upstate is holding for the four athletes who lost their lives plus the lone survivor.

I immediately begin to say a little prayer for Felicia. We didn't know her but my heart is hurting for her. I just can't imagine the pain and suffering she must be enduring physically but, mainly mentally and emotionally. Her family is flying in from Sweden and I empathize with her and the agony her parents are enduring. Knowing your child is injured and to be so far away from her bedside has to be overwhelming. I also begin to pray for the other parents as well. They are enduring the loss of their children too. I pray for strength for them. I also say a little prayer for all the classmates and teammates of all five athletes, the professors and administration of USC Upstate for the upcoming days and months. This accident would leave an everlasting impact on the USC Upstate community.

## OPEN

Open your eyes and you will see me there.
Open your ears and you will hear me there.
Open you heart and you will feel me there.
Open your soul to God to allow him to heal your sorrow there.
Open your mind to God's grace and I promise I will be there.

## THE RUNNING SHOES

There is a pair of running shoes that is lying within your room.
These shoes journeyed with you on the grassy hills of
Milliken and USC Upstate every day.
For it was those shoes that felt every bit of your grace,
your determination, your struggles, and your faith too.
It was those shoes that got you where you were going.
For you are now the good Lord's to keep.
As I hold those shoes I am reminded of you.
The tears begin to flow down my cheeks.
For I know these shoes were upon your feet.
I pray and ask why? Why Him Lord?
I miss you dearly as I continue to weep.
The Lord must have wanted you to run the streets of gold.
For maybe that is the reason He called you home.
But, now the Lord has bestowed upon you a perfect set of wings.
The running shoes will forever be a reminder of my son
who left his imprint upon everyone he met.
Those imprints left an impression that no one will ever forget.
The running shoes will always remain lying on your floor within
your room.

# CHAPTER NINE
## *The Candlelight Vigil*

W e arrive at USC Upstate's soccer fields and I am flabbergasted by the number students, professors, athletes, friends, and family members who are here to show respect and mourn the loss of four beautiful souls. I mostly see a community coming together. I hold on to Johnny and Macy is beside me. The rest of our family and closest friends stay with us too. USC Upstate Chancellor Moore and Tammy Whaley greet us and quickly shuffle us into a ballroom of sorts. As we walk in I notice the media off to the side. I also notice people lining up to sign booklets that rest on four podiums.

Once in the ballroom, Tammy hands each of us a white t-shirt with #SpartanStrong printed on the front. She also hands us a round sticker with my baby's beautiful face on it. It is Josh's athletic picture. His big, beautiful smile is gleaming and those eyes are staring back at me. I quietly take a seat and begin touching Josh's face on the sticker. Tears are forming in my eyes when I am touched on my back. It is James' aunt and she hugs me tightly.

"I am so sorry. So, so sorry," she tells me again and again.

She introduces me to James's parents, Emily and Shawn, and we embrace. Yes, I am mad at their son but at the same time I am heartbroken for them, too. They have lost their oldest son. Their baby is gone, too. The pain that Emily and Shawn are experiencing is probably just as bad as the pain Johnny and I are enduring. Johnny and I also got to meet Mills' parents too but didn't get to meet Sarah's parents.

As we wait to be escorted to the stadium, I see a round table covered with stickers that bear the faces of Josh, James, Mills and Sarah. I pick up several stickers of Josh. I want to hold them close to my heart. Each of us is given a green ribbon to wear. We pin it to our chests, to represent the university's colors. We all wear it proud and true. Everyone who fills that stadium that night wears a ribbon.

Chancellor Moore leads us outside and all I hear is complete silence. The four families are seated at the top of the stadium in reserved seating. A slight breeze is blowing and it is so quiet that you could hear a pin drop. Sobs are the only noise that cuts across the silence. Looking out over the soccer field, I see Mills' and James' team numbers painted on the field in their memory. Several people are seated on a small stage in the middle of the field. Sam Cheshier is among those seated on the stage. He is going to speak for Josh. Sam plays soccer for USC Upstate so he also knew James and Mills.

Johnny and I sit side by side just staring at the stage. My heart is breaking for all the students and fellow athletes who are impacted this tragedy. USC Upstate will never be the same as of October 11, 2015. The entire stadium is full and the athletic teams are seated on the grass at the edge of the stadium. The chancellor steps up to the microphone and address the people who fill the stadium. His eyes are red from crying. He shares kind words of encouragement to the families but mostly to the students. He ends his speech with "we always will be Spartan Strong."

Sandy Vang, the student body president, speaks next and she shares her deepest sympathies and prayers with all the families and her fellow classmates. Her words touch my heart when she says, "I asked my father why bad things always happen to good people? He responded with, "When you go into a garden, what do you do? You pick only the best rose. That is what God does. He only picks the best."

Sandy's message really touches home for me. God does only choose the best. Josh, James, Mills and Sarah will always be remembered for the way they led their lives. Yes, all five students who got in that car on that autumn night made the wrong decisions that affected five families' dynamics forever. This accident changed a university, altered friendships and athletic teams too. But, they were good kids. Period! I become emotional and at that moment set my mind on not letting anyone speak harshly about these kids but especially not about our Josh.

The students who are speaking begin talking about their fellow classmate, teammates but mostly their friends who they have forever lost. They all share stories of how James, Mills, Sarah and Josh touched so many lives just by their personality, work ethic and strength. Sam is the last one to speak. As he talks about Josh, he is crying and being consoled by two other athletes. We are hurting for Sam and I want to run down the field and walk upon that stage and finish his speech for him. Sam has lost his best friend and two fellow teammates. He bravely tried to pull his friends from that burning Mustang and cried out when he could not save them. He watched his best friend die and is haunted by the images from that fiery crash. I immediately begin to say a prayer for Sam and the two others who so bravely helped him at the crash.

Several people have assembled at the side of the stage and they are holding dove shaped balloons. All of a sudden one balloon escapes and starts to float above the crowd. It just hovers over the soccer field.

Johnny nudges me with his elbow and says, "There goes Josh."

This makes me laugh. Josh was always first in line or the first to be ready to go somewhere. Why should tonight be any different? Josh was always excited about a new adventure and now he had the greatest adventure anyone could ask for. Josh was on his way to Heaven I thought as I watched the balloon move over the tennis courts.

That lone balloon had hovered over the soccer field for James and Mills before hovering and staring over the tennis courts for Sarah. The wind carries the balloon on the exact path that Josh took on his runs to Milliken where the Spartans cross country team compete.

I bow my head and cry. They are leaving us forever. My baby, my Josh, our Josh is gone. My world is unraveling again.

Each athlete's life is represented by that one lone balloon. Each day the world will bring us new challenges. We must face each one head on. Gradually our lives ascend towards the Heavens. Further away from our lives here on earth. The balloon is out of eyesight of the loved ones they leave behind. This just proves that life is fragile. So, live your life everyday like it is your last because one day in an instant it will be.

The chancellor speaks again and a prayer is said. The administrators begin lighting everyone's candles. The entire stadium grows quiet and somber. Again, sobs break the silence.

Johnny and I hold our candles watching the yellowish orange flame flicker in the night. Once everyone has extinguished their candles, we are escorted inside where the crowd of mourners swarms Johnny and me. All of Josh's teammates come to speak with us and there isn't a dry eye in the building. One female athlete, who loved Josh dearly, is crying so hard that Johnny is literally holding her up. At that moment, I realize how much everyone at USC Upstate loved and adored our Josh.

Two young men approach me and ask, "Are you Josh's parents?"

"Yes we are," I tell them.

I am Micah Burnette and this is Andrew Richard," one young man begins telling us. "We were the ones who helped get Josh out of the car."

I grab Micah and hug him tightly. Tears are falling down my cheeks and I tightly hug Andrew.

"Thank you. Oh my God, thank you so much. I cannot thank you enough for helping get our Josh out," I cry to Micah and Andrew.

I interrupt Johnny's conversation to introduce Micah and Andrew. Johnny shakes their hands and hugs them both. Like me, Johnny is so grateful to them both for their heroic actions. They will always hold a special place in our hearts. I introduced Micah and Andrew to Macy and watch as she hugs and thanks them. I want desperately to ask Micah and Andrew about the accident but I know it will be painful for them to relive the sequence of events again and I don't want that pain for them. Like Sam, they saw and experienced horror that will forever remain with them.

Several of Josh's professors approach Johnny and me to introduce themselves. They are or are so choked up that speaking is next to impossible. One professor has crafted a writing pen for us using the hardwood that was once was USC Upstate's basketball court. He did this because Josh had once served as a referee for the intramural teams and he thought Josh was a great and wonderful person to all the athletes and students who participated in intramurals. That was our Josh. Josh would attend almost every sporting event on campus to support his fellow classmates and athletes. Josh treated everyone on the USC Upstate campus as equals.

Another professor came up to us and gave us a pinned button in memory of Josh who was in his teaching cadet class. He chokes up talking about how Josh encouraged others and how Josh was so loved and adored by the kids, teachers and parents at Spartanburg Christian Academy. He told us that Josh really interacted with the kids and played on their level.

The crowds were beginning to disperse and I searched for more stickers of Josh. I don't find any. They are all gone. Not one single sticker of Josh can be found anywhere. I ask Tammy Whaley if she knows where I can find more but she tells me they have all been taken.

I am stunned. My Josh, our Josh was loved by so many people. This outpouring of love, shown to us but mostly for Josh, is evidence. Josh is the only student who is from Spartanburg killed in the crash. People living in Spartanburg County and surrounding areas and the USC Upstate campus want to show their support. A tragic accident has claimed the lives of four vibrant college students. This doesn't happen in Spartanburg. This accident has hit home for everyone.

Our family is escorted to our cars and we all leave the campus heartbroken but, mostly honored. We are proud to know that so many people loved our beloved Josh. It is evident by the hundreds of people who attended the candlelight vigil. As we drive away from the campus, I turn my attention to the sky searching for the lone balloon. We pass Milliken and I try in earnest to catch one last glimpse of that dove-shaped balloon but all I see is an empty field and a memory of a runner who would no longer compete for the school he loved.

Johnny, Macy and I head straight to bed when we return home. We are mentally and physically exhausted. Tuesday is going to be extremely difficult with Josh's visitation and seeing him lying in a casket. We just want privacy and rest for a few hours. Thankfully, we sleep for a few hours.

## IT WAS ONLY A DREAM

You came to me in a dream today.
You called out my name and said, "Mama I am okay."
You had a sparkle in your eye when you gave me your perfect smile.
You reach for my hand and said, "Mama I am okay."
You had a white shimmering glow surrounding you as a sense of peace
came over me. You hugged me tight and said, "Mama I am okay."
You told me you have seen us cry and heard our plea's
to God to tell us why?
You wrapped your arm around me and told me the answers will be
revealed in all good time. Then you said "Mama I am okay."
You sat down beside me as I gently and preciously touched your cheek
and rubbed my hand through your hair. You said, "Mama I am okay."
You told me how beautiful Heaven was while you held my hand and
wiped away my tears.
You said, "Mama I am okay.
You told me how much you loved us and were watching after us
from Heaven above.
For I shouldn't be sad and that you couldn't stay.
You kissed me goodbye upon my cheek.
Then you said, "Mama I promise I am okay."
But, I was awakening with a jolt. Tears of happiness and sadness came
flooding over me.
For I knew that God sent you to me to tell me you are okay.
You are okay!
It was only a dream.

## THE EMPTY BED

All I see is an empty bed of my child taken way too soon.
The sun beams in with its rays resting upon where you use to lay
your precious head.
Your room is filled with all of your memories.
Your treasures from your adventures, your toy trucks, your
books, and your picture.
If I listen closely I can still hear your laughter in a faint whisper.
I still can smell the scent of your cologne when I hold your
pillow.
Your clothes are hanging just like you left them.
Your shoes are in the floor.
I can feel your presence as I begin to cry.
I begin asking why Josh, why?
I close my eyes and you are there.
Smiling at me with that beautiful smile.
You kiss my cheek and you tell me not to worry because you are
with Jesus and perfectly okay.
I opened my eyes and you are gone.
I replace your pillow as I continue to weep.
I turn to leave and close the door and there lies a penny.
For it's a simple reminder that you will always be there.
I went into your room today.

# CHAPTER TEN
## *To See Our Josh for the Last Time*

It is Tuesday, October 13, 2015 and Johnny and I awake at 6 a.m. We shower and try to prepare ourselves for what today will bring. The thought of seeing our son, our Josh, lying in a casket just unnerves me.

"We shouldn't have to do this," I tell Johnny. "This is all wrong and backwards. We, the parents, are expected to die first not the other way around."

I grab my little wooden cross and head to the kitchen to grab something to drink. I am so nauseated that I can't eat anything.

"I just want some sweet tea," I tell Lisa who is in the kitchen. Macy is still asleep. I take my tea and little wooden cross and return to my refuge on the front porch. The air is a little chilly and there is a light breeze blowing. I sit in the rocking chair and watch the sun rise higher into the sky. I ponder what today will be like.

As I watch the birds, a big ole bumble bee flies around me. Every few minutes it flies right up to my face and I swat it away. The bumble bee is persistent and I laugh as I think of Josh trying to scare me to death with bugs. I remember a time when Josh was seven or eight years old and I heard him and Macy laughing in the living room. I was cleaning my bathroom and bedroom but every few minutes I would hear footsteps enter my bedroom and then run back into the living room. I hollered out, "What are y'all up to?"

The only response I get is giggles. Walking out my bedroom, I see the biggest bug I have ever seen in my entire life. I scream bloody murder and jump on my bed. Josh and Macy are rolling on the floor in laughter. Josh picks up the bug and I am mortified.

I screaming at Josh, "Put it down. Kill it, son! Kill it!"

Josh laughs and pets that big bug like it is a pet or something. Josh gets on the bed with me and I scoot backwards trying to get away from the bug.

Josh laughs and says, "Mama, it is just a fake bug. Gotcha!"

"Seriously, son. You about gave me a heart attack," I tell him. Josh loved playing jokes and pranks on me. I am so gullible. That boy always knew how to push my buttons.

Sitting on the porch, I begin to smile. I look up towards heaven and thank God again. He knew I needed to smile and laugh again. He helped me remember Josh who was so precious, hilarious, and who loved to aggravate the snot out of me. I am going to miss Josh so much. The jokes, the pranks, the gotchas!

At 8 a.m., my sisters and Mom are back at the house. Lisa has picked up Jo. Johnny is watching TV but, I know he is really deep in thought about Josh. Like me he was still in shock that we have lost our son. I sit down beside him and hold his hand before putting my head on his shoulder to cry. We don't need words. We are feeling the same anguish and heartbreak over the death of our Josh.

Tara Revels, one of our dear friends, drops off bagels and cream cheese. Her two sons attended Broome High School with Josh where they played football together. She held me tight as I told her what had occurred over the last two days. Tara told me she is praying for us. I could see the fear in Tara's eyes as she silently imagined losing her two sons as she imagined the loss that Johnny and I are enduring. Nobody should have to experience such an unimaginable loss. I thank Tara for her visit and the bagels. I am able to eat half a bagel and can tell I needed it.

The morning hours slowly pass as peace lilies, floral arrangements, mums of every color, and huge variety baskets of different flowers were delivered to my home. There are 30 to 35 floral deliveries and I read every card. There are even saplings and bushes, garden statues, bird houses, and yard flags delivered to our house to create a memory garden for Josh.

By 11 a.m. our house is full of family and friends. I stay on the front porch in my rocking chair. The weather is perfect with a clear blue sky, sunny and warm with a slight breeze. My dog Bentley, who is a mix of Shih Tzu and Maltese, sleeps in my lap. He loves to rock with me on the porch. It is amazing how animals can detect sadness or that something is about to happen. Macy is rocking beside me. I flash back to Saturday night when Macy was sitting at the bar in the kitchen doing her homework. Josh's cat Snickers is a 15 pound Calico who is very temperamental. It's her way or the highway persona.

At around 11 p.m. that night of the accident, Snickers kept jumping on Macy and interrupting her. Snickers jumped on Macy's laptop and pawed and meowed like she wanted something. Snickers has never behaved this way before. Macy and I thought Josh's cat was hungry or going crazy so I feed her in the garage. Did Snickers sense that something was going to happen to our Josh, her Josh? Did she try to warn us? Snickers loved her some Josh and always stayed by his side when he was home.

"Macy," I screamed, scaring her to death and, bless her heart, causing her to jump from the rocking chair.

"What Mama? What is wrong?"

"Think how Snickers acted Saturday night. She knew Macy. Snickers knew Josh was going die," I say between deep sobs. Macy is beside me and we hold each other for a few minutes.

Johnny comes out to the porch and says, "It is time to go to the mortuary."

We were meeting Courtney and her mom, Ciara Murphy aka "Vegas", the Bryson's, the Jones', the Crocker's, Sam Cheshire, and Josh's roommates Sam Moss and Rinaldi at the mortuary. Jo decided not to go and stays at our house with her friends. She wants to remember Josh the way she knew him not by seeing him in a casket. Jo doesn't handle death or illness of a loved one very well. It was her choice not to go to the mortuary. If she couldn't handle seeing Josh lying in a casket then she did the right thing by not going.

Seeing my child lying in a casket is going to be the hardest thing I've ever had to. I begin praying and squeezing that little cross over and over.

"Please God, help us do this. Please," I say all the way to mortuary as I look out the window of Johnny's truck. I admire the blue sky as I try to catch a glimpse of an angel, a sign, any sign that Josh is still with us.

By the time we reach the mortuary, I am tearful again. Courtney and her mom are already here along with our family, close friends, and Sam and Josh's roommates. Mr. Dunbar's secretary greets us. I go straight to Courtney and hug her. She is so nervous. We all know how hard this is going to be on each other. To actually see our Josh lying in a casket was tortuous. There aren't enough words in Webster's dictionary to describe our emotions and anxiety as we sat together in the mortuary.

Mr. Dunbar escorts Johnny, Macy, and me back first along with my mom, my sisters and their husbands, and Lisa to another room. Once there I knew my Josh, our Josh is just behind the sliding doors. Mr. Dunbar has Josh's pictorial slideshow playing along with music.

"Be strong, Laurie. Be strong," I tell myself and I grab hold of my cross and squeeze it tightly.

Mr. Dunbar explains to us, "Josh made me work hard. He is somewhat swollen. When you see Josh, please don't apply pressure when you touch his face and head."

Johnny, Macy and I are going to see Josh first. Mr. Dunbar slides back the doors and as soon as I saw the casket I see Josh's face. I feel a knife stab me directly into my heart.

I don't mean to but loud wails escape me. Johnny holds me around the waist to keep me from falling to my knees.

"Johnny, it's our baby. Look at our baby boy."

"I know, Laurie. I know," says Johnny. He is crying just as hard as Macy and I. We both cling to Johnny's arms.

Mr. Dunbar takes us closer to Josh and I ask him, "Can I touch my baby?"

"Certainly."

Johnny, Macy and I stand over Josh with tears streaming down our cheeks. Complete emptiness falls over us. I place my right hand over Josh's heart, wishing and pleading for this not to be real.

"I love you, son. Mama is here, baby," I tell Josh as I rub my fingers through his hair and touch his precious lips. Josh doesn't look injured lying in his casket. His neck is swollen on both sides. Josh looks like he is just sleeping, but, my heart knows otherwise. This is his shell. His soul is in Heaven.

I gently rest my lips upon his cheek and kiss my baby boy goodbye all the while sobbing and grieving for my son.

"Wait on us, Josh. Wait on us," I whisper to him as I run my fingers over his beard. I can't stand his beard but that makes him Josh. I lay my hands over his and gently rub his crooked left pinky finger. I moved over more so Johnny and Macy can say their goodbyes.

"Son, why? Why, Josh," Johnny repeats and he bends down and kisses Josh on the forehead and holds his hand. I have never seen Johnny cry like this as he tells his only son, his namesake, goodbye. Johnny hardly ever shows his emotions and I am hurting for him. I want to take all this pain away for him and Macy.

Macy has the visor that Josh always wore, his PlayStation controller, and her coroner's investigators badge. She wants these things placed in the casket with Josh. Josh told Macy how proud of her he was and how "cool" it was for her to be a coroner investigator. She wants him to hold onto her badge for eternity. Macy stands over her brother and cries uncontrollably. She has literally lost her best friend. Macy and Josh were as close as siblings could be. They told each other everything. They valued each other's opinions and were very protective of one another.

I stand there beside my son gently rubbing my right hand through his blond hair. All three of us are sobbing as we stand there in silence.

"It is not right for a father and mother to have to look down upon their child in a casket," I cry. "This is not happening. Dear God, please take care of my, our Josh. He is my baby, God. Please!"

At that moment anger takes over my body. I am mad at the world. I want to scream and holler. I am mad at God.

"What kind of God takes a person's child? Why Josh? Why our Josh?"

I am mad at James for driving so recklessly. I am mad at Felicia for surviving. I even wonder why it can't be Josh who survived. All these questions are rushing in and I want them to stop. I grab my cross and hold it tightly again. I immediately become calm and under control. I ask God to forgive me for having these thoughts. I would never wish any harm to anyone. I am just not that kind of person.

Mr. Dunbar asks us to step out of the room for a second. Josh is leaking fluid again from his right ear and Mr. Dunbar needs to fix it before the rest of our family and friends see him. We step out in the parlor and I am crying so hard that I can't talk. I see my mom first. I want my mom. I am 48-years-old and I want my mother. She grabs me and holds me as I weep in her arms.

"Mama, my baby is gone. Mama, my baby is gone."

Everyone is crying now. I guess seeing Johnny, Macy and me so visually distraught automatically confirms this nightmare is real.

Mr. Dunbar reopen the viewing room for our immediate family to see Josh. Johnny goes with Lisa while I stay in another room with our closest friends. I sit down beside Courtney. Hugging her, I tell her that Josh looks okay. I hope this relieves some of her anxiety. I feel so sorry for her.

"Bless her heart," I keep saying to myself as I see the pain and nervousness on her face.

Sitting there beside Courtney waiting for her to go back to see Josh, I remember the stories they told us on the beach this past July. Courtney described when they first started dating and Josh took her around Spartanburg showing her where he grew up near Dorman High School and then around Broome High School. Once Josh was taking her back to the USC Upstate campus and Courtney had to go to the bathroom. Josh kept driving around Hearon Circle just to aggravate her. Courtney made it to the bathroom at her apartment but, that moment had her falling more and more in love with Josh. Josh never put on a fake persona or pretended he was someone other than himself. He had the love him or leave him attitude. Why? Because that was our Josh.

It is time for Courtney and Josh's roommates to see Josh. Johnny and I gave them privacy by staying in the lobby to watch the video of pictures that will play during visitation tonight and at the funeral tomorrow. I catch myself smiling and giggling at one point. Everyone there thinks I have lost my mind but I don't care. Seeing these pictures of Josh smiling and being goofy brings a glimpse of joy to me. They are several photos of Josh in his childhood years, his glory days at Broome High School, and of him running in his USC Upstate jersey with his snow white bird legs glaring. Some photos have his crazy facial expressions. There are pictures of Josh and Sam being Josh and Sam, and pictures of Josh and Courtney together. Every picture has Josh smiling and loving life.

Josh lived everyday like it was his last. He smiled and laughed from the moment he woke up until the time he went to bed. He would randomly burst into Amazing Grace or an off the wall song, which the lyrics had no meaning. We knew Josh was home or nearby because we could hear him coming. Everyday Josh faced the world head on. No obstacle was too big or too small for him. So, these images I am viewing of Josh bring me joy. I have joy knowing my son lived everyday like it was his last. My son loved unconditionally and my son laughed every day. There aren't too many people who can say that about themselves or their child. But, Johnny and I can bear witness to this truthful fact.

I walk back towards the viewing room where Courtney, Rinaldi. Sam M. and our Sam C. are saying their goodbyes to Josh. I watch as they cry and hold on to one another. Looking at them, I witness the bond of unconditional love and friend-ship they had with Josh and they have with each other. Mr. Dunbar sees me and I nod that it is time to escort them out.

Johnny, Macy and I go back to see our Josh's body for the last time. I kiss Josh goodbye on the cheek and say, 'I will see you later, baby. Wait on us, son. Wait on us. Give Daddy a hug for me, okay? I love you Joshua!"

Johnny kiss him goodbye and so does Macy. We leave that room sobbing and not wanting to let him go.

## PEOPLE

People keep telling me to be strong that you are always with me.
But, in my heart I feel you embedded there
But, my soul wants you here.
People keep telling me to hold onto the memories we shared
together.
But, that's all I have now
since we can longer make new memories together.
People are moving on with their lives. Smiling, laughing, and
rejoicing.
But, all I can feel is guilt and complete emptiness knowing you
cannot laugh or smile with us.
People say our grief will ease in time.
But, time is all we have now.
Day by day wishing you haven't went away.
People were put in our lives now and that I can witness.
It's the people who have helped me be strong.
Helped me make new memories to share.
Helped me smile again.
But, time is what I need.
Time.
Precious time.

# I'M ALWAYS THERE

I'm always there
Just don't make a sound and listen closely
For I will be the beat of your heart
The whisper of the wind
The warmth of the sun radiating down
The moonlight gleaming across the sky
The delicate wisp of the wings of a butterfly
The joyous sound of a songbird
The raindrops bouncing around
Just listen for my voice
It will always be embedded within your heart
I'm always there.

# CHAPTER ELEVEN
## Visitation of Friends

We leave the funeral home to go back to our house. Lisa has the video to play during visitation. We ride all the way home in silence. All this silence is killing me. I turn up the radio. I can care less what was playing. I just want noise to distract me for a while. We arrive back home and our yard and driveway is filled with cars again. I notice more flowers have been delivered along with bushes and trees for us to plant. A birdhouse engraved in memory of Josh is also there.

Our kitchen counters overflow with food and casserole dishes. My dining room table is covered with every kind of dessert—cookies, cakes, pies, brownies, cheesecakes, and cupcakes. The entire back wall of the dining room is lined with paper products that are stacked two and three feet deep in some places. Five coolers in are garage are loaded with soft drinks, Gatorades, waters, and ice.

Macy plays the video for Josh's visitation and everyone stands around watching it. Johnny is outside and I am so exhausted that I just want to sit down and catch my breath. I sit there for 30 minutes before the nervousness kicks in. I stand up and go to the kitchen for a drink. My oldest sister is in the kitchen with about 20 people. I turn around and my house is full of people again.

I stand beside my breakfast bar and just watch people's facial expressions. Some have smiles on their faces while others just keep their heads bowed. Others have tears falling down their faces while some are deep in conversations. A few people nod in agreement while others shake their heads back and forth to answer no. I just stand there lost in a trance.

Tammy gets my attention and says, "Laurie! Laurie, I have a line of people here to speak with you."

"Okay. Where are Johnny and Macy?"

"Johnny is out back. Let everyone come through the front door and speak with you then they can go outside to Johnny outside and work their way back towards the front yard. This will help keep the line moving."

By the time I can tell Tammy that I want Johnny and Macy beside me, the line has begun. Nearly 600 people come to pay their respects and they keep saying, "We are so heartbroken for y'all. If you need anything, please do not hesitate to call or ask."

I hug everyone that comes to our house and thank them with my whole heart.

As the crowds ebb and flow, they all assure us that Josh is in Heaven. Some tell us stories of how Josh changed their lives, befriended them, or how his contagious smile had them at hello. Others remarked how much Josh looked like Johnny or how he kept them laughing. That was our Josh. He always wanted you to be happy. Josh hated to see someone cry or look sad. Even if a stranger was crying he somehow would make them smile by talking with them.

Several of Josh's teammates tell us stories about Josh. They talk of how Josh would randomly burst into Amazing Grace, prank someone, or just tell a funny joke. They made me laugh as they described Josh to a tee. One young man told me about when Josh was dared to stop at a field during practice. A mean bull was in the field and Josh was to aggravate the bull. So, Josh stopped and stood on the fence and while screaming, "Here kitty, kitty, kitty!" The bull ruffed and charged at Josh who let out a wail, "Run! Run! It is after us. Run!" The teammates heard and saw the commotion and all of them took off in a full sprint. The bull was running along aside of them inside of the fence. Once everyone was safely away they all began running in laughter, even Josh because of his antics. That was our Josh. Never was there a dull moment if and when Josh was around. This story made me laugh because I pictured Josh aggravating the fire out of that bull. I could even see him screaming at his teammates scaring them too.

Another story was about the cross country team at their annual eye-opener competition in Spartanburg at Milliken Park. It had been pouring down rain the night before and early in the morning hours on a cool fall day. None of the runners wanted to run because of the misery of running in the cold rain. Needless to say everyone got through it. Back on the bus to go to USC Upstate everyone was dripping wet and freezing. Our Josh stripped down completely naked to change into something warm and dry. He turned around with a straight face and told his team, "Don't look unless you want to see two tic tacs!"

I respond with, "Bless!" Bless is all I can say because that was our Josh. He wasn't ashamed or even embarrassed. He was a very truthful person. If a thought entered his mind it exited through his lips. Once again Johnny and I laugh. Only our Josh could have thought of that to announce to anyone in hearing distance on that bus that day.

It is 8 p.m. when Coach Smith and Matthew Johnson stop by. Matthew is a former USC Upstate cross country runner who now works at the university as a videographer. He used to run with Josh and he presented Johnny and me with a picture of Josh at his last cross-country meet at Winthrop University. Josh has on his white USC Upstate jersey and his green running shorts. Josh has a determined facial expression. The picture is so special because Josh has a pair of life- like angel wings; well to me they are real now. Once I see this picture, a flood of emotions rush over me. I gently hold the picture and outline the wings with my finger. No words are exchanged but, everyone there knows how much this means to Johnny and me.

To see our baby boy, our Josh running with a perfect set of wings confirms that Josh is now and will always be our guardian angel. Josh will be running the streets of gold but, rest assure he will be laughing and bringing joy to all the angels now. I ask my sister Tammy to email this picture of Josh to Dunbar Funeral home. I want it displayed when the song When I Get Where I'm Going plays. This picture will illustrate that Josh's journey here on earth is done but, his journey to Heaven is just beginning.

I also tell Tammy to email the picture of Josh with his arms stretched open wide on top of a mountain. Josh is grinning from ear to ear in this picture. He posted this picture on his Facebook page with, "On Earth there is no Heaven but, there are little pieces of it!" This photo will be displayed as Josh is taken out of the sanctuary for his last ride while the song See You Again plays. I believe this is a perfect way for everyone to say goodbye to our Josh and yes, to tell Josh we will see him again once we get to Heaven.

Our house begins to settle down around 9 p.m. My family

and closest friends stay and try to clean up the kitchen. We pack up more food for Josh's fellow athletes and Courtney and her roommates. We don't want all this food to be wasted and we know these kids will enjoy it. Johnny and I finally sit down and I proceed to write everything I plan to say about Josh at his celebration of life ceremony. It takes me about an hour to write it all down as if I am telling a story. I name it Our Josh.

Josh was our baby boy. Johnny and I want his celebration of life to be about him and not our sorrow. We want people who didn't know Josh to catch a glimpse of "Our Josh." For those who already know "Our Josh," we want them to remember and understand why everyone loved him. It was Josh's laughter, his smile, his sense of humor, his love for mankind, and his love for his family and friends. This is the hardest thing I had ever had to do besides letting my baby go on October 11, 2015.

## THE DAY YOU LEFT

The day you left us our hearts broke into.
Every day we try to be strong it is just so hard to do.
It's your beautiful smile I see when I awake and it's my last thought
before I fall asleep.
I sit and wonder what heaven is really like.
As I stare across the fields and watch the birds play and take flight.
I replay your song day after day. For it's a remembrance that I will
"See you again".
I long to hear your voice and to hear Mama one more time.
I see you everywhere I turn.
I search for you in the crowd but I am left abandon with
only your memories.
They day you left us I kept saying it's only a dream. This is
only a dream.
Please be only a dream.
Realization set in and the nightmare comes true.
You are gone.
Never returning home.
Reality!
For the day you left us our hearts broke into.

## I WILL SEE YOU THERE

I reached out for you
But, are not there.
I call out your name
But, you do not answer.
I heard your name called
But, I couldn't find you in the crowd.
I heard you laughing and saw your face
But, it was only a dream.
I heard Mama being called
But, I turned to respond and it was for someone else.
I begged you not to go
But, you chose to follow the Lord home.
You looked back and said, " Don't worry, I promise
I will see you there!"

# CHAPTER TWELVE
## *Josh's Celebration of Life*

O n Wednesday, October 14, 2015 Johnny and I wake up knowing our baby boy, our son, our Josh will be laid to rest. We lie in bed holding one another. Again, we exchange no words. We both know exactly how the other one is feeling at this exact moment in time. Our hearts are completely broken as tears stream down our cheeks that leave a proof of our grief upon our pillows.

Johnny gets up first and showers. I take Bentley outside and Lisa is already up. She has woken up Macy for me. While Bentley roams around the yard, I take my seat in the rocking chair on the porch. I look up at the sky and notice the vibrancy of the blue sky. A few clouds sporadically float by as a light crisp breeze blows. I feel the chill that fall brings to my skin.

A few birds fly above me and some land on the ground singing their joyous song. They hop around searching for a treat to start their day. A rustling of the leaves in the tree lines catch my attention and I search in earnest for the reason behind the noise. I know it is a deer but, it stays hidden among the foliage of the trees. Bentley comes back to the porch and jumps on my legs wanting me to pick him up. I grab him up and kiss his soft fuzzy little head. My love of this precious little fur baby is comforting to me.

I know it is time to get ready so I slowly walk to my bedroom. Johnny has showered and is putting on his black suit. He always looks so handsome in a suit. The pain, brokenness, and profound deep hurt he sustained to his own heart are displayed on his face. I know his heart is breaking. Johnny is so much like Josh. They both always smile and are full of laughter. But, today Johnny wears his heartbreak on his face.

I hug Johnny and kiss him on the cheek. Taking his strong hands into mine, I say "He loved you Johnny. Josh loved us. We will get through this, right?"

Johnny doesn't respond but, his eyes give me his answer. He tries not to cry. Johnny hugs me and leaves the room.

I shower and dress in my maxi black dress and a jacket that Ms. Sheila has loaned me. The jacket has the exact color scheme as USC Upstate. I want everyone to dress in black and green—USC Upstate's colors—to celebrate the love and passion Josh had for this university. I ask USC Upstate students to wear the school colors and any student athlete to wear their dress sweat suits. I think Josh would like us honoring him this way.

I take a deep breath and join the others in the living room where we wait for the family car to take us to First Baptist Church of Cowpens. This is where we will say our final goodbyes to our Josh. All of our immediate family is here and I am aware of the multiple conservations taking place in hushed tones.

Johnny is sitting in his usual chair watching television. Macy is still upstairs while everyone else is gathered in the kitchen, sitting at the bar, or sitting at our dinette table. I pour a glass of tea to calm my stomach. I don't know why I am so nervous. Maybe it's just the thought of putting my son down into a six foot hole or never seeing him again. I sit down beside Johnny and patiently wait.

Soon I see the family car making its way up our long drive-way. We leave the house in silence. Johnny, Macy and I sat in the front row while my mom, Lisa and Jo sat in the back row. My sisters Tammy and April and their husbands Mark and Terry along with my nieces and nephews follow behind us in their cars. Courtney and her mom will meet us at the church where Courtney will sit with my family. She was going to be our daughter-in-law one day so it only seems appropriate she be beside us today. Johnny and I hold hands and are silent on the ride to the church. My mom, Lisa and Jo carry on a conversation but I don't listen. I just want quietness.

As we near the church, the abundance of cars parked along the side of the road catch my attention. We see hundreds of people walking towards the church where they will pay their respects and help us pay tribute to our beloved Josh. I am in total awe. The intersection where we turn to reach this church is blocked and a policeman is directing traffic. The policeman is trying to help people find parking spaces and to get the family car to the church.

The family car finally makes the left turn and I see it. A hearse is parked in front of the church. I am sickened with grief as I realize my son's body is in that hearse. I lower my head and plead with God, "Help us do this. Help Johnny, Macy, and me. Please! Please give me the strength to speak on behalf of Johnny and Macy."

The driver takes us to the back of the church where Mr.

Dunbar's staff escorts our entire immediate family to a Sunday school room. There we wait to be brought into the sanctuary. I know that's Josh's casket is in the sanctuary. I sit in the hard plastic chair and read my notes. When I talk about Josh, I want people to understand and to witness for themselves how wonderful and how loved our son was. As we sit in that small room, I try to find the courage to paint pictures with my words to share Josh's extraordinary life.

Mr. Dunbar enters the room and tells us the 400-seat sanctuary is completely full. "The gym is also full. We have created an overflow room with a monitor and speaker so they can at least hear and see the funeral."

Mr. Dunbar and Preacher Westafer estimate that more than 700 people are attending Josh's funeral. This is an amazing testimony about how many lives Josh touched. The magnitude of how much Josh was loved is on display with family, friends, fellow athletes, classmates, professors, teachers, customers, and total strangers who have come to pay tribute and to celebrate his amazing life.

It's now time to enter the sanctuary and Johnny grabs my hand. Macy and our family follow us. As we enter the sanctuary, I see our closest friends the Brysons, the Jones' and the Crockers. Johnny and I look to the left and there is Josh. He casket is draped with the USC Upstate flag and there are several floral arrangements around him. A breathtaking 16x20 photo of Josh in a suit sits on an easel beside his casket. I look up to see the picture of Josh with his arms opened wide and smiling his beautiful smile. Johnny squeezes my hand tightly as we sit down. My heart breaks for Johnny. He is already crying and the service has not even begun.

I comfort Johnny the only way I know how by patting him on his back. His whole body is shaking and he sobs loudly. I am the one who usually needs comforting but, today it is Johnny's turn. I am here in presence but, not in a mindset to grieve for my son. Instead, I focus on not crying.

"You will not cry Laurie. You will not cry," I tell myself repeatedly.

The sanctuary is filled with love for Josh and we can feel it where we sit in the front pew. The warmth embraces us. The sunlight gleams through the stained glass windows with prisms of colors were reflecting around the sanctuary.

"God is with us. He is here in this sanctuary," I tell myself as I feel calm or maybe God put me in trance to ease the burden of heartache for maybe just a little while.

Preacher Westafer approaches the podium and gives thanks to everyone for attending Josh's Celebration of Life ceremony. He speaks of Josh's favorite bible verse Philippians 4:13, "I can do all this things through Christ who strengthens me" (NIV) before going into prayer.

"God please be with Josh's family and with us. The shock of losing Josh is monumental and seems more than anyone can bear. May Josh's loved ones find faith in Him and be comforted. For our Christian bonds will bind all us together in our need of sorrow and mourning," prays Preacher Westafer.

He then nods for Coach Frye to come to the podium to give his eulogy of an athlete.

## "SEE YOU LATER"

You left us here on earth.
We don't know what to do, how to act, or even know what to say?
Everyone is missing you more and more on each single day.
We know God took you to be with Him for some reason unknown.
For we have finally realized you are no longer with us or
ever coming home.
Our grief for you son cannot be written, described, or can
even be discussed.
We sit and stare at your pictures just hoping and wishing you would
just walk through the door.
Then the heart wrenching sense of loss reestablishes itself within our
thoughts and hearts again.
Our tears begin to flow down our cheeks as we weep for you my son.
Your room has the presence of stillness and memories of your life.
We know you are waiting on us to arrive at the gates of Heaven.
So, son enjoy being on the right side of God.
Until that day comes when we get to see you again
We will dream of seeing your sparkling baby blues.
We will be dreaming of your contagious laughter and your
infectiousness smile.
We will be dreaming or your warm embrace while you kiss us
upon the cheeks.
But, mostly we will be dreaming to hear your sweet voice again.
Baby we will always love you but we will never say good bye.
For it will now and always be,
"See you later."

## TIME

Minute by minute, hour by hour, day by day we still wished you
haven't went away.
We wished we had more time with you.
Time for more laughter, time for more smiles, time for more talks,
time to just hold your hand.
We would trade all of our time to just to hug you again,
to hear you voice, to hear your laugh, touch your face,
and even wipe away your tears.
We lost our time with you on becoming a teacher, marrying your
love of your life,
your children, and our time with just being with you.
Time will escape us while your time has become an eternal rest.
All awhile you are overlooking on us from high above.
Time stood still the very moment that our Heavenly Father called
for you to follow him home. The momentary serenity was present
in that hospital room as the Angels surrounded you.
For there is one thing that time cannot ever take from us and that is
our love for our child.
For our love is everlasting and will never abide.
It is now just time. Time is what only separates us.
For we have faith that we will see you again. It's only in a
matter of time.
His time.

# CHAPTER THIRTEEN
## A Coach's Tribute to an Athlete

Coach Skip Frye walks up to the podium where he shares his story about a former student, an athlete, and a cherished friend who could change your perspective about life just by knowing our son Josh. Coach Frye is somber and struggles to address us. His voice cracks and he chokes up while expressing his deepest and cherished memories of everyone's Josh. As Coach Frye speaks there are awes, some sobbing but, more importantly there are spurts of laughter echoing throughout the sanctuary.

Coach Frye tells us, "Johnny, Laurie, and Macy, I am honored to have the opportunity to speak of Josh; a young man of such loving and compassionate, and high character... but also a character! When Johnny asked me to say a few words about Josh, I decided to look to God's word for a little guidance along with the traits of Josh. Two days ago, in the bright sunshine,

Johnny, Laurie and I spoke about Josh's exuberance for living life to the fullest every single day. Just look at the picture on the handout. It's like Josh is saying, "I want as much of today as I can get."

A verse jumps out at me and I have to look it up. Psalms 118 matches Josh's enthusiasm for living. "Today is the day the Lord has made; Let us rejoice and be glad in it!"

I don't think I ever saw Josh when he was not enjoying and rejoicing life to the max. Whether it was a prep rally, practice, lifting weights, or working with his daddy at the station, Josh rejoiced in living! And that rejoicing rubbed off on those around him.

Josh helped us to rejoice in the gift of every day as well. His smile helped many classmates and I know it helped some teachers get through a tough day. He probably saved a dozen or so lives of teachers. I know his friends and teammates will always remember that smile or his little jokes when he greeted you. Josh helped us to rejoice in the gift of every day as well. He sure brought a smile to the track coaches face every time he came down the hill to practice.

Josh's good and solid friend Sam spoke of Josh's unselfish nature. That alone epitomizes Josh. How true! Let me say that the value of a man's life does not lie in the length of his life. The value of a man's life lies in the relationships and the care he shows for others. In Philippians, Paul tells us, "Don't just be interested in your own affairs, but be interested in others in what they are doing." Josh cared for those he was around. He went out of his way to encourage the smallest, slowest seventh grader on the team just as much as the one that scored the most points!

Just recently at a meet, I heard two stories about Josh's caring nature. Josh and his teammates volunteered on a Saturday at the Eye Opener XC. The Junior Varsity race was the last race of a long day. It's a time when most 20-year olds are looking for the quickest chance to leave. A runner at the back of the pack finished and Josh treated him like he had just set a course record, congratulating him and high fiving him. That kid and his father told me how important Josh made him feel that day.

"It was amazing that a college runner would even think enough to want to do that. But, Johnny and Laurie, Josh did that to everyone."

A Broome High School runner told me that when she was in the eighth grade, she told Josh she was not going to run track because she wouldn't be any good. First, I can't believe anyone would say that about track. Josh, at the time was a senior, gave her a little cross and told her it would be her good luck charm for the season. She was so excited that a senior athlete like Josh would even recognize an eighth grader that she did run and did succeed. I bet many of you have a "Josh" story just like these because… hey that was Josh!

Two teachers at Broome told me stories of Josh. Pam Flynn of the teacher cadet class said that Josh kept the class going all the time until finally she asked Josh to help her calm the class down. Also, Ms. Kingsland, the art teacher, once sold pop tarts as a fund raiser. At graduation Josh and Ms. Kingsland sat beside each other. Josh bumped her knee and said, "Ms. Kingsland, I am so nervous, do you have a pop tart?" (the entire congregation all laughed) That was Josh.

I have been really lucky in my days to have coached many of good kids. A number were faster than Josh. But, I tell you, I never coached a better kid than Josh Lee. I was excited when he asked me if I thought he could make the track team at Upstate. I know Upstate and the Spartans have been blessed by having Josh out there. I know he loved being a Spartan! So, thank you Upstate for taking Josh into your family. I was even more excited when he decided to be a teacher/coach. You just knew he would be the teacher/coach you hoped your son or daughter would have.

Johnny and Laurie, Josh and Macy are testaments to the type of parents you are. I know how important it was to Josh to make you proud. He and I talked about that often. And I have seen you beam with pride as he grew into as fine a young man as I have known. I know too, that God has met Josh, seen that bright smile, and told him, "Well done, my good and faithful servant." Thank you.

Coach Frye returns to his seat and several videos of Josh being Josh play for the congregation. Laughter is all I can hear. That was Josh.

Gia Diamaduros begins singing Amazing Grace acapella and is joined by Gary McGraw on piano. Her voice is truly angelic and it brings tears and chills to everyone as they listen to the words. I hold my cross and stare downward for seeing Josh's face on the screen will cause me to break down. Amazing Grace was Josh's favorite gospel song and he would often just burst into the lyrics no matter where he was or who he was with. That was Josh.

## AN ANGELS SISTER

I am sorry I had to go my sister.
I wanted to stay but God called me home on that October day.
I had to tell you my sister that I will miss you the most.
I'm going to miss our talks, our laughs, and even our pillow fights.
I know I am not there but please be assured that I will be checking
in on you.
So please keep an eye out for our mom and dad.
They are so sad and I understand.
But, help them realize to give their grief into Gods hands.
My sister please don't cry any more tears.
For I am one of God's Angels that can actually fly.
I actually sit beside the highest of Kings of Kings.
I fly high with the eagles and jump between stars.
I can even sing.
My sister now you go live your life and follow your dreams.
I am still and will always be so proud of you.
You will always be my sister and I your brother.
My older sister you can exclaim that you have a brother
unlike any others.
You can voice that you have a guardian angel
because you my sister was and will always be my inspiration.
Love you Macy!

## HEAVEN'S WEDDING

There will be a wedding once you get to heaven.
After you see Jesus you will see me.
I will be the one wearing angel wings.
I will be standing up front with all our loved ones for you to see.
You will be wearing white and a smile that is so bright.
Your beauty will recapture my heart for you knew all along you had
it from the start.
There will be the most beautiful flowers draped all around
With pearls and diamonds cascading down
While the Angels sing their joyous sound.
There will be a wedding in Heaven
but, only in God's good time.
I will be waiting for you to journey down the aisle.
At that moment the church bells will chime.
As we finally get to say I do!
For I have always loved you.

# CHAPTER FOURTEEN
## *Courtney's Josh*

Courtney begins her testimony on Josh by addressing the Upstate athletes and her friends for being there for her during the worst time in her life. Courtney has not only lost her best friend and soul mate but, also lost three other fellow athletes and friends. Courtney thanks Johnny and me for raising an amazing son with whom she fell in love. The sanctuary is filled with laughter, sobbing, and "awes" as Courtney shares stories of Josh.

The following is the exact words that came from her heart and soul:

"The first time I met Josh was in our Religion class. The first day of class he sat two rows over from me and out of the corner of my eye I kept catching him glancing at me. The second day of class Josh had moved over and was sitting in the desk next to me claiming that someone had stolen his empty seat. It took two weeks for Josh to instant message me on Twitter and say, "Hey. I hope you don't think I'm a stalker or creepy but what's up?" It took about a month for me to finally cave in and agree to go on a date with him. He tried to take me to Applebee's and have "like" an actual date but I made him drive separately and meet me at Moe's. The date only lasted like 30 minutes and he never let me forget that I picked that place because, if things weren't going great I could ditch the date fast.

I was so hesitant to go on a second date with him but, Josh was so persistent that he was going to make me his girlfriend. He seriously fought so hard to get me and I can truly say I have never had anyone care for me the way Josh did. I was trying to think of what to say as I stood in front of you all and the only thing that I kept hearing from everyone was "you knew the other sides of Josh, you knew him better than anyone." At first I felt guilty for people saying that to me but, then it made me want to share those parts of him with all of you.

Everyone that knew Josh knew that his smile could light up an entire room, his laugh was contagious, and you definitely knew what if felt like to be loved unconditionally. Nothing was casual with Josh and you could hear him from a mile away. Josh was everyone's go-to person. He was the guy everyone called when their car wouldn't start and you were stuck in the rain trying to jump a car with broken jumper cables. He was the guy that would hug you out of nowhere and not let you go even if you tried too. Even on your worst day he was the one person that could make you feel like everything was going to be okay; it was a constant reminder of the big picture of life and all of the beauty rather than the small things that are less important. He was the guy that put life and laughter into every situation.

My favorite memory I have with Josh is a night that we spent sitting in his truck. We had gone to dinner for a friend's birthday and had ended up getting in our first argument. Instead of being mad and not talking to one another we ended up sitting there holding hands talking about God. He opened up about his insecurities and began to share his testimony with me. That night he told me that he had been saved at a Young Life Trip and it made my heart so happy. Sitting here today knowing that He accepted Jesus as his savior and knowing that he is up in Heaven puts the biggest smile on my face. We made a promise to each other that night that we would never go to bed mad at one another and I can't express how impactful that was on our relationship.

One of the things I loved the most about him was that he would wink at me every time he saw me. It was almost like a game between the two of us, except I can't wink so he just made me look like an idiot. Although Josh joked about marrying my best friend and running off to Vegas with her, his countless fake proposals still got me every time. Whether it was warning me about a ring I might bite into while eating or making me turn around when he was on one knee simply picking something up, I got butterflies each time because I was confident that one day it would be real. Josh made me feel like the most important person in his life. We would be out in public together and he would yell across a room at me and say "Hey girl, your momma let you date?"

We took a ski trip with some friends last winter and from the ski lift he yelled "Hey you in the white jacket, "lemme" get them digits?" The entire ski mountain looked at me like this kid has lost his mind if he thinks he could use that as a pick up line. If that wasn't bad enough, Josh was the worst skier I have ever met and literally tumbled down the bunny hills. But it was moments and sayings like this that make me miss him the most. We dated for almost a year and a half and yet he made me feel like every day he was seeing me for the first time.

I am pretty sure that if I got up here and didn't share this story with you guys, Josh would be disappointed so here it goes: The Infamous Naked Mile: Josh was at a bonfire at the track team's house and was of course being the life of the party. He was playing a game with some other kids and made a bet that the loser had to do a naked lap around the house with everyone watching. He of course lost the game and within seconds he had stripped down butt naked and took off in a full sprint. He came up on the first turn and his ankles got stuck in his boxers and he completely wiped out. He somehow scrambled up on his feet still with his hand covering everything and ran across the line yelling lets goooo! I wasn't there to see it but, everyone knew my boyfriend as the naked mile guy. He was the only person that would be willing to do this without second guessing it but, knowing that it would make people laugh was worth it to him.

I could probably go on for hours about how much Josh meant to me but, I hope this allowed you guys to see the Josh I got to fall in love with. I can't express how much love I got to experience with him but, there will always be a huge spot for him and his amazing family in my heart. I'll miss riding around in your truck, going to Bruesters and getting cotton candy explosion ice cream with rainbow sprinkles, looking up at you and having you kiss my forehead, and more than anything miss you saying "I love you".

He tweeted a few months ago "I'm not striving to make my presence known, but instead my absence felt." If that doesn't sum up what were all feeling today, then I don't know what does."

Everyone applauds Courtney. She and Vegas walk toward their seats and I stand up and hug her.

"Thank you and we love you, sweetheart," I whisper to her.

"You are welcome and I love y'all too," she says.

I sit down and Johnny is still crying. I try to comfort him as I refuse to cry and swallowed my tears back down.

"Stop it, Laurie! Stop it! You will not cry," I tell myself.

Gia sings the Lord's Prayer and her angelic, amazing voice fills the sanctuary. All heads are bowed as the lyrics were praising God and giving thanks to Him. There isn't a dry eye in the house. Johnny is literally shaking and my sister wails out, "I can't do this." Gia ends the song and everyone in unison says, "Amen!"

## NEVER GOODBYE

When you proudly walk across that graduation stage
please stop at the end and point towards the sky.
For James, Mills, Sarah and especially me will be cheering you on
because we never got to tell you goodbye.
I have checked on you from time to time.
I have even kissed you on the cheek and even sang "Hakuna Matata"
while you were fast asleep.
I am so proud of you and please keep smiling your beautiful smile
and to laugh again
because your laughter is what will always
brighten my day.
You go follow your dreams and please never give up.
Enjoy your life and live happy and free.
I promise I will be waiting on you patiently.
I love you Courtney to the end of time.
For it was your beauty and grace that captured my heart.
For you knew all along you had it from the start.
Till I see you again
but, it will never be goodbye!

## SHADOWS

There are shadows.
Everywhere I turn is a shadow.
Everywhere I look I see your shadow.
Shadows of your blond hair and baby blue eyes.
Shadows of your smile and infectiousness laugh reflecting
off your portraits.
Shadows of your passion for mankind and determination to prove
your self-worth.
Shadows of your generosity bestowed upon strangers.
Your mark forever embedded in their hearts.
Shadows of your ability to brighten a room with your presence.
To bring laughter into a depressed world.
Shadows of a son, a brother, a grandson, a boyfriend, a friend, and a
nephew ricocheting through our thoughts.
Shadows of an athlete's determination to Finish the Race.
To never give up! Striving to complete the task.
Shadows of all the memories you left behind.
For that is all we have left.
Your memories.
Your shadows.
Shadows.
Everywhere I turn is your shadow.

# CHAPTER FIFTEEN
## *Our Josh*

It is now my turn to speak. Josh was our baby boy. Johnny and I want his celebration of life to be about him and not our sorrow. We want people who didn't know Josh to catch a glimpse of "Our Josh." For those who already knew "Our Josh," we want people to remember and understand why everyone loved him. It was Josh's laughter, his smile, his sense of humor, his love for mankind, and his love for his family and friends. This is the hardest thing I have ever had to do besides letting my baby go on October 11, 2015.

I stand up and a hush fills the entire sanctuary. I can feel everyone's eyes upon my back as I walk to the podium. My eyes fill with tears and I hold my cross and ask God to help me do this for Josh. I was shaking as I began to speak. I keep my attention on Johnny then to the person I am speaking of during my testimony. Soon I become calm and I am determined to finish without crying. I want laughter because Josh was all about bringing laughter into this depressed world. Giggles and the full blown roar of laughter is what fills the church during my testimony.

My words are a mother's love for her son.

"To every parent out here, to every child out here, tell your loved ones you love them every night because that phone call may come and you don't want it. My Josh would not want me to cry so, he would be hollering down at me, "Laurie Anne, Stop It!" Johnny, Macy, and I want to thank everyone who has called, texted, sent flowers, brought food, or who has come by the house to pay their tribute to our precious Josh. There are not enough words in the dictionary to express our gratitude of the outpouring of love given to us from friends, family, co-workers, and total strangers but, mostly to the USC Upstate family. We will be forever being indebted to you all. I wrote this last night and it is called "Our Josh."

Our Josh loved each and every one of you dearly. His friends, family, and his faith were what made Josh, well Josh. I've said it before and will say over and over, "If you knew love you knew my Josh, if you knew laughter you knew my Josh." Laughter is what made my baby who he was and what he will be remembered by his friends and family.

Josh out of the blue would commence into a song with absolutely no harmony because, that was Our Josh.

Josh would just break into a dance without absolutely any rhythm. He didn't care because, that was Our Josh.

Josh would just pick on me and push my buttons just to get me "riled" up. All the while winking or tapping Johnny's, aka Pops, shoulder just to get my reaction. That was Our Josh.

Josh would answer my calls by saying, "What you want woman or what you want Laurie Anne?" Why? It was because that was Our Josh.

Laurie Anne would be yelled back after I would say, "Throw down your clothes." That I knew I just washed them because Josh couldn't tell what was clean versus dirty. Why, because that was Our Josh?

Our Josh had a contagious smile that would warm your heart, because that was Our Josh.

Our Josh had your heart and friendship at hello or more specifically at 'What's Up?" It was because that was Our Josh.

Our Josh always made his presence known when he entered a room or you knew Josh was there because you could hear him before you actually saw him, Period! Why? It was because that was Our Josh.

Our Josh wasn't scared to be first in line or be more determined to first in line when food was involved. That was Our Josh.

To Josh's classmates and especially his teammates at Broome High School and Upstate: Our Josh loved his classmates and teammates with every ounce of his being. Treasure those moments and never forget Our Josh. Our Josh was a fierce, fierce friend to all because that was Our Josh.

To his roommates Rinaldi and Sam: Thank you from the bottom our hearts for putting up with stinky socks, Josh's chicken in a can concoction, and his recipes for chicken out of a can. But mostly helping Josh by being his partner while he learned the Salsa. That was Our Josh.

Our dearest Courtney: Josh loved you more than the world full. You were his soul mate and his universe. Even though he would pretend his was proposing but, in Josh's heart he really was. Courtney the moment Johnny and I met you we knew one day you were the one who our Josh was going to marry. Even though he would tell you to stop complaining…That was Our Josh. In all seriousness, Our Josh loved you with every fiber of his heart and soul, my sweet girl.

Our dearest Sam Cheshier: Your friendship with Our Josh was truly shown on October 11, 2015 the moment you helped my baby out of that car. Johnny and I will forever be grateful to your heroic actions to save our son. Yes, you two were our entertainment especially at the beach. At this nice seafood restaurant when you two were pretending to be having an argument, in the parking lot, in Spanish that neither one of you could speak. Everyone was staring and was pointing for someone to do something. People were standing up and down in total disbelieve on what they were experiencing. Sam, also how you and Josh were constantly playing out the movie scene from Forrest Gump from upstairs. You were portraying Jenny with a muffled sound saying, "Forrest, Forrest," and Josh screaming, "Jenny!" Why, because that was Our Josh.

My dearest immediate family: Our Josh loved us and showed us his love and laughter every day.

Johnny you were his hero and his life. He looked up to you and he was proud of the man he had become because of you. He loved me. Only time he called me Mama was when he was sick, needed money or he was hungry. But, I will always be his Laurie Anne.

From picking on you Jo or to Josh "Fro Nanny," or aggravating you Lisa constantly making you say, "Stop it Josh!" Why? Because that was our Josh.

Making you April riled up about 911 calls or Tammy making you wonder with total frustration, "What?" Nanna making you laugh and say, "How mercy!" Why, because that was Our Josh.

Mr. & Mrs. White, even though you are not blood, you were Josh's grandparents. He loved you just as much he loved his own. For that Johnny and I will be truly grateful.

Our dearest Macy: Our Josh and you were and will always be your Dad's and also my heart. We are proud of both of your accomplishments. Even though Josh and you had your sibling fights but, y'all always would makeup because that was our Josh. You know your brother loved you because he was constantly giving you "food" money. But, you are so like me that money burns a hole in our pockets and Josh is just like his daddy. Both can stretch a penny into a dollar. Because that was our Josh or maybe it was the Goodwill Store. That was Josh for you.

In all seriousness, Our Josh was about laughter, love, and living every moment like it was his last day here on Earth. Johnny and I can honestly say that Our Josh accomplished his goal of bringing laughter into our lives, loving every one unconditionally, and just living by sharing his gift of bringing joy to the world.

To my baby Josh: You are now our angel above watching over every one here today in this sanctuary and for those who were unable to attend. We know you are in Heaven teaching Jesus and all the other angels, along with your grandfather's, on how to make chicken in a can concoctions, sing and dance to your own style of harmony and rhythm, and how to make sure they always laugh. Because of your smile and laughter and undying love for mankind you were and will always be OUR JOSH!"

## MY FATHER'S SON

The day I was dying Daddy I could hear you there begging God not
to take me away.
I know you feel abandoned and if I had any other way
I would have spared you Daddy your unbarring pain.
But, Daddy my eyes were upon Jesus as His angels were escorting
me away.
It was to my final destination on that October day.
You raised me to be faithful and true.
To always work hard and to be strong just like you.
You encouraged me to follow my dreams Daddy and never give up.
For it was you Daddy who was my hero all the way up to
my journey's end.
I was so proud to be your son.
Because it was your strength and honor that made me into a man.
You taught me how to live but mostly how to love.
You taught me to show respect and how to honor my
friends and family.
I have been watching over you from up in Heaven above.
I have seen your tears and can hear your pleas.
It is okay Daddy.
I am where I need to be.
I send you my love everyday Daddy.
Just look for my signs.
It will make you laugh and smile.
For it is what you need to heal your heart.
Just give it a little time.
For I will always be my
Father's son.

Preacher Westafer speaks of Josh's time here on Earth for 20 years, 1 month, 18 days, and 8 hours. He speaks of Josh's accomplishment and how Josh was to begin teaching this past Monday as a teacher cadet. He speaks of two enduring images of Josh. Josh always smiling and Josh being surrounded by friends. He speaks about the shock everyone here today is experiencing.

Preacher expresses trueness and how Josh was a true testament of a follower of Christ. He preaches from the book II Timothy 4:7, "I have fought the good fight, I have finished the race, I have kept the faith." (NIV) He also speaks of the book of Acts 20:24, "However I consider my life worth nothing to me; my only aim is to finish the race and complete the task the Lord Jesus has given me-the task of testifying to the good news of God's grace." (NIV) Preacher expresses how you cannot finish or win a race by looking over your shoulder but by looking forward. Keep the faith. He talks of how Josh was carried to heaven by angels. His reward would be given to him by Jesus Christ. That Josh ran his race; Josh kept his faith and is ready to receive his award.

The preacher ends his remarks and the picture of Josh running in his Upstate jersey and having his angel wings is displayed on the screen. When I Get Where I'm Going by Brad Paisley and Dolly Parton begins to play and the congregation is silent except for sniffles and sobs. I believe everyone pictures Josh as each lyric of the song is sung. The lyrics are such a harmonious replica of how everyone pictures Josh as he entered Heaven and got his well-deserved wings.

## ON ANGEL WINGS

What is it like to be angel my child?
Is it like soaring with the eagles throughout God's painting in the sky?
What is like to be an angel my child?
Is it like the peacefulness of a stream trickling down the mountainside?
What is it like to be an angel my child?
Is it like a brilliance of color that is illuminated from a rainbow after a
thundershower?

What is it like to be an angel my child?
Is it like floating on a gentle breeze during the summer throughout the
countryside?
What is it like to be an angel my child?
It is the softness of the cottony, fluffy clouds configuring shapes
for all to see.
What is it like to be an angel my child?
For I get to fly to you at night to let you lay on my angel wings
to provide you protection and peace while you sleep.
For theses wings are the everlasting symbol of the bond and love
between a parent and a child.
For this is what it is like to be an angel
It's a gift from high above.


The song ends and Preacher Westafer dismisses us in prayer. I look up and see Josh on the screen again with his bright smile and his arms opened wide. The song Wiz Khalifa—"See You Again," featuring Charlie Puth, "Fast and the Furious 7 Soundtrack," starts to play and it is beautiful. All of sudden the song breaks into rap music and I am mortified.

"Oh, Lord they are playing rap music in church," I think before it hits me like a brick wall. Josh got the last laugh on his Mama.

I am smiling ear to ear and I look up towards heaven and tell Josh, "You got me baby. You win!"

Mr. Dunbar ushers all the Upstate athletes, row by row, out to the sidewalk where they line up all the way up to the hearse. He directs the pall bearers who carry Josh to the hearse with us following. The rest of my family and friends follow row by row. The song continues to play as we leave and is just perfect as it signifies Josh's last ride and the bond he had with everyone that will never be broken.

## ANGEL'S EYES

I see the world through my angel's eyes.
Through my angel's eyes I see no more hate
But, unconditional love for humanity.
For my angel gave love without the need for any in return.
Through my angle's eyes I am unable to see the color of skin or
social class now.
For all I see is an individual demanding to be treated as equals.
For my angel would encourage your voice to be heard.
Through my angel's eyes I am able to seek out a stranger in need of
a companion in Christ.
For my angel brought friendship to a lonely heart unselfishly.
Through my angel's eyes I am able to see the glimpse of joy that
each day brings.
For my angel knew laughter is what blinds a depressed world.
Through my angel's eyes I am able to see the strength of one man
To overcome his insecurities because he never gave up hope.
For my angel knew that his faith will enable him to succeed.
Through my angel's eyes I am able to see the beauty of this world.
For I no longer see the ordinary.
I can visually see the vibrant paintings of God's creation.
For my angel knew that beauty is within your inner soul; you just
have to look deeper within yourself to find it.
I see the world now through my Angel's eyes.

# I WENT TO YOUR GRAVE TODAY

I went to your grave today.
We had a conversation about life and why you had to go away.
I was crying as I laid the flowers upon your name.
There was a peacefulness surrounding me as a moment in time came to
a standstill.
I had a sense of you holding my hand
As tears began to cascade down.
The breeze was gentle and light.
As I saw a silhouette of you kneeling down and you were smiling ever so bright.
For you wiped away my tears while I looked at your beautiful face.
You had the most magnificent angelic wings.
I hugged and hugged you and kissed your cheeks.
As I spoke and cried out how much we have missed you.
You spoke to me in a clear, soft voice.
Telling me Mama I promise everything will be alright.
You described how Heaven was such a beautiful place and how you are in the
presence of God's amazing grace.
You talked about seeing the streets of gold and how Heaven is a sight to behold.
You talked about Jesus and how he hugged you on that October day.
You said He will be with us every step of the way.
Just keep our faith and give our grief to Him to hold.
You told me you see and hear us crying for you every day and asking God why?
You promised all I have to do is just kneel and start to pray.
For He is the only one that can take our pain away.
You assured me that it's just your body in that grave but, your soul is what made
you, You.
For you will be within our hearts as long as we keep saying your name.
You kissed me goodbye and assured me that I will be with you again and that
your love for us will always be steadfast and true.
I told you I love you my son as you drifted away.
I went to your grave today.

# CHAPTER SIXTEEN
## *Graveside Service*

We follow Josh outside the church and watch as the pallbearers lift his casket and take him to the hearse. The entire side walk is lined with all of Josh's Upstate's cross country and track/field teammates and his roommates. I notice their faces. Everyone is crying. Tears fall from their cheeks. My heart aches for them as I realize this is the first death many of these college students have experienced. They stand there alone, lost in their grief.

I hug Rinaldi and Sam M. before Johnny, Macy and I are shuffled back into the family car. Sitting in the car and watching the pallbearers place Josh into the hearse is my breaking point. I finally start to cry and I can't stop the tears. I hold Johnny's hand and squeeze it tight when I see that he is teary too. We both silently stare out the window while my mom and Jo have their own conversation.

Every direction I look I see our friends, family members, Josh's friends, classmates, teammates, and strangers walking towards their cars. The hearse starts moving and we follow it. The police car has the intersections blocked again. All the way to the cemetery I keep my eyes focused on the back of the hearse where my baby lies in a casket. My mind races while my heart breaks.

The family car pull into the cemetery but it seems like it an eternity before we reach Josh's gravesite. A tent shades the six foot grave where our only son will be laid to rest. We remain in the family car and I see people gathering around the tent to say their last and final goodbyes to Josh. The pallbearers line up behind the hearse to lift Josh's casket from it. As they place Josh over his grave Mr. Dunbar opens the door to the family car and escorts us to Josh's gravesite.

Numb, Johnny and I just stare at our son's casket. Our Josh was in that wooden box. Preacher Westafer begins speaking about laying our son to rest. It was a short service on the committal to the Earth to ensure the resurrection into eternal life, through our Lord Jesus Christ. After Preacher Westafer says the prayer of eternal life, Mr. Dunbar and an employee walks up to Josh's casket and begins to fold the Upstate flag that was draped over his casket. We used the flag to show homage to our son and the university for which he loved whole heartedly.

Mr. Dunbar walks towards me where he kneels down and hands me the flag.

With tears streaming down my cheeks, I look up at him and say, "Thank you so much."

I place my hand softly over the flag before bringing it toward my heart and hugging it with every ounce of my being. Johnny places his arm around my shoulders and he cries with me. Johnny places his other hand over my heart where the flag rests and we just sit there holding the flag. We know how much

Josh loved attending Upstate and what this flag now represents to us.

After Johnny and I regain our composure each pallbearer comes up to us. One by one each pallbearer hugs us and tells us how much they love us. Josh's teammates follow and we hug and cry with each of them. The blessing we receive from these students, athletes, and everyone in attendance is truly heartwarming. Family and friends form lines to speak with us and somehow Johnny and I get separated.

When the lines of people near the end, I go and stand at Josh's casket. My hand is on top of the casket and I pat it. I cry because I don't want to leave Josh there.

"I want my son back. I want this nightmare to end so I can just wake up," I think to myself. The nightmare is real and isn't going to end as I realize my son will be placed six feet in the ground and there is nothing I can do to bring him back to us.

"It's time to go," I hear someone tell me.

I move to the end of the casket where Josh's head lies and I kiss the casket again and again while hugging a wooden box.

"I love you, son," I say over and over and plead to God once again to take care of my baby.

Chelsea and Brittany, friends of Macy's, help me back to the family car. Johnny, Macy, my mom, Jo and Lisa follow us. I just want to go home and be alone to grieve for my son. We leave the cemetery knowing that within minutes Josh will be buried. This is his eternal resting place.

As young children, I always told Josh and Macy to sleep sweet. As the family car drives away from the gravesite, I look back and say, "Sleep sweet baby boy, just sleep sweet." No one else heard me but, Josh did. I know he did.

Our entire family is at our house for lunch that First Baptist of Cowpens has provided. Johnny, Macy, and I are finally able to eat a little something. Friends still come by to see us throughout the day and the house is finally empty around 8 p.m.

It is just three of us now. Our family of four is now three. Our journey of grieving for Josh has begun and it becomes my mission to learn what actually took place on Fourth Street on October 11, 2015 at 1:45 a.m.

## SLEEP SWEET JOSH

Sleep sweet my son
Sleep soundly and tight.
Sweet dreams my son
With dreams all through the night.
Run swiftly my son
Run and play.
Laugh and smile my son
For that is what brightens the day.
Ride on snowflakes my son
For each is as unique as you.
Take flight with the angels
Sing and dance too.
For perfect harmony and grace is now bestowed upon you.
Illuminate the sky like the fireflies at night
For your light will forever shine so bright.
Your time on Earth was cut too short
As we had to say our final goodnights.
Your legacy will always be known
While you sit beside God on His throne.
So sleep sweet my son
Sleep soundly and tight.
Sweet dreams my son
Dream of us tonight.
Just sleep sweet!

# SHOWER OF TEARS

I'm crying showers of tears.
Trying to conceal my crying.
Crying deep inside because losing my son is at
the forefront of reality.
My exterior is just a facade of the emotional turmoil
my heart is enduring.
I can feel the gut wrenching sensation churning upward
demanding release.
Tears are forming within my eyes wanting to blind my vision by the
floods of emotion.
Fighting the urge.
Swallowing them back down determined not to cry.
They are relenting to overpower like a storm releasing
its power upon the earth.
I fall to knees as the storm of grief increase in strength
I am overtaken by its power.
The tears overflow the flood gates, falling rapidly down my cheeks.
The wail of mother crying over the loss of her child.
Echoing up and down the halls.
For the showers of tears has left me alone with a torn, broken heart.
For I am crying a shower of tears.

# CHAPTER SEVENTEEN
## *The Fight for Toxicology Results*

Johnny, Macy and I try to learn the new "us" and adjust to life without Josh. Everything changes again on November 24, 2015 when Johnny and I are called to Spartanburg County Coroner's Office to go over the toxicology reports. Coroner Rusty Clevenger and his investigator, who was appointed Josh's case, escort us to a conference room where I notice a huge folder on the table. It takes everything in me not to grab up the folder and flip through the pages.

"Thank you for being here today," the Coroner tells us. "I am so very sorry for your loss."

Johnny and I both say, "Thank you."

He opens the folder and brings out a single piece of paper. He looks at Johnny and then at me.

"Josh's toxicology report was completely negative. Josh had absolutely nothing in his system. This is something to be proud of," he tells us.

We look at the official report and I notice an alcohol level of 0.016%. The level of alcohol to be considered lawfully under the influence is 0.08%. As a nurse and the daughter of a Spartanburg County Sheriff's Deputy and a professor at the South Carolina Police Academy who specialized in defensive driving and DUI awareness, I know that Josh's level for alcohol was the equivalent to washing your mouth out with mouthwash or it could have been what he ate prior to the accident. My late father never missed an opportunity to tell his kids and grandkids about the danger of drugs and alcohol.

"What can you tell us about the driver's toxicology results," Johnny asks.

"I have to release the results to his parents first but then I can share it with y'all," Coroner Clevenger tells us. "The media is aware that the results are back and they will probably be contacting us."

I am fine with the media contacting me because I want to stop all the rumors that my son was drinking under age.

We thank the coroner; say our goodbyes and Johnny and I both return to work. I tell my co-workers that Josh's toxicology results are negative and we will know the driver's results once James' parents are notified.

I return to seeing patients. After lunch I receive a phone call from the coroner.

"One of the decedent's parents has objected to the release of toxicology results because they feel the release of toxicology results is a violation to the HIPPA law," he explains that the toxicology results are part of the autopsy record and releasing the information to the media or individuals not associated with the investigation of the case is in violation of the HIPPA law. "The media is all over this and probably will try to contact you or Johnny."

"So, you still cannot tell me the driver's levels yet," I ask.

"No ma'am. Not until the South Carolina Attorney General determines if this breaks HIPPA laws and this may take several months," he tells me.

Overwhelmed I begin to sob and can't speak. Debbie tries to calm me down so I can tell her what is wrong.

All I can say is, "The media. The media is trying to find me. It is happening again. The drama will not end Debbie."

She calms me down a bit and I can finally tell her the news. The doctors and the rest of staff try to convince me to go home but, I know I am safer here at work because the media isn't allowed on hospital property. Within the hour my phone is ringing non-stop with reporters wanting my statement about Josh's toxicology reports and my opinion on not releasing any of the decedent's blood alcohol levels. I call Johnny and let him know about my conversation with the coroner. We are both mad because we have every right to know if the driver was under the influence when our only son was killed.

As I pull into my driveway I receive a text back from Courtney. I had texted her earlier to give her heads up that the media wanted a statement. Courtney was on her way home to North Carolina for the Thanksgiving holidays.

"Have you heard any news on the driver's toxicology results," I ask her.

"Yes. James' parents already told the soccer team that his blood alcohol level was 0.122%," Courtney tells me.

I immediately become hysterical. I walk into the house I grab my little cross and hug it.

"Why, God? Why Josh," I say out loud which brings Macy running down the stairs.

"Mama, what's wrong? What's wrong," she asks and I sit on the couch crying uncontrollably.

Johnny arrives home and comes straight to me and hugs me. "What's wrong, honey?"

"He killed our baby, Johnny! He killed our baby! Johnny, why? Why did this happen?"

I am sobbing so hard that I soak Johnny's work shirt with my tears.

"I don't know, honey. I just don't know," Johnny tells me through his tears.

I finally calm down enough to tell them what I knew. I think that after hearing the truth of my son's accident, reality struck a chord with me. I am finally able to admit that Josh was killed in a car accident. My Josh is gone because of a careless, reckless, and selfish act that could have been avoided. Josh knew better than to get in a car with someone who had been drinking. So now, Johnny and I will be grieving for our son until the day we both take our last breath here on Earth.

As days and weeks pass we have to endure our first holidays and our birthdays without Josh to celebrate with us. There aren't enough words to describe the feeling of loss on special holidays and special days without your loved one beside you. The empty chair syndrome is what I call it. Johnny and I did not have the strength to cook and celebrate Thanksgiving at our house so our entire family ate at the Marriott Hotel. My birthday is the day after Thanksgiving and I miss having Josh to sing his version of Happy Birthday in his baritone voice. I spend my birthday at home with Johnny and Macy. I don't need a present or birthday cake. What I want for my birthday cannot come from a store.

It has been our family tradition to celebrate Christmas with both sides of our families and to host Christmas Day dinner. As Christmas Day approaches, I am not in the holiday spirit and cannot bring myself to decorate the five trees that usually adorn our home. The only tree I can manage is a white Christmas tree decorated with green, black and white ornaments. It's an Upstate tree and I call it Josh's tree.

Christmas morning is very upsetting for us. There are no presents under the tree for Josh. His stocking is not filled with surprises. However, I do include Josh's name on the gifts under the tree. From: Johnny, Laurie, Macy and Josh. I signed ALL our names because I was determined not to leave Josh out. But, the reality of Josh not being with us dampened our Christmas spirit.

We visit our only son at his grave site on Christmas Day. The marker still hasn't arrived so Johnny's mom places a Christmas tree and I place roses on his grave. Johnny and I stand over Josh's grave mourning him on what should be a joyous occasion. We can't find happiness amidst our grief. Looking back in hind sight, Josh did get to celebrate Jesus' birthday in Heaven. There aren't a lot of parents who can say this but we can.

As night falls, I sit outside on the porch wrapped in my fleece Sherpa throw looking up at the stars. I talk to Josh as if he is sitting beside me. My tears flow as I ask him questions. This is when I become bound and determined to finish Josh's race. An inner voice keeps saying to me, "You can start a campaign to save another life by being a witness of God's word and by giving a detailed version on what exactly happened on October 11, 2015. You can also share with the world how Josh's legacy left a lasting mark and how it is still changing lives. I will succeed."

## MY CHRISTMAS WISH

If I had a Christmas wish it would be
that a very special angel
could come down from Heaven and  spend Christmas with me.

We would decorate the tree and wrap the presents with
ribbons and bows.
While the fire rumbles and crackles
as the embers illuminate a breathtaking glow.

We would make cookies and drink hot chocolate too.
I would even put in extra marsh mellows
like my angel would always do.

We would all sing Christmas carols in a tune
that only my angel knew how to do.
Then we would all burst into laughter when we got through.

We would go sledding and make snow cream too.
We would all sit by the fire and read *'Twas The Night
Before Christmas*
as my angel would play out the scenes that only he would
have the nerve to do.

I would fix all his favorite foods and sit around the table telling
stories of  how my angel brought joy and laughter
into everyone's heart every single day.

My angel would tell us it's time for him to go as he starts to
ascend back to Heaven.
He hugs and kisses us goodbye.
Then he looks back and promises that Jesus and He
will always be by our side.

I plea for my angel to stay
but he stops and turns around with his wings opened wide and says
Mama I promise I am ok.
I will always be with you.
All you have to do is say my name.

My wish for Christmas.

## STAR LIGHT

Star light, star bright,
First star I see tonight,
If I may, if I might
Make a wish upon you tonight.
The wish I wish is simple as can be
It is for one of God's angels named Joshua Lee.
Star light, star bright,
First star I see tonight,
He loved to laugh, he loved to sing.
He would bring laughter and joy into everything.
Star light, star bright,
First star I see tonight,
He had a kind spirit, and a heart of gold
For that is something that only God could bestow.
Star light, star bright,
First star I see tonight,
He had the bluest of eyes and a smile that would brighten anyone's
day.
For he knew the cross was the only passageway.
Star light, star bright,
First star I see tonight,
The wish I wish is for the angel to know
For He will be sorely missed and forever loved.
So bless him with God's amazing grace until the day I finally get to
hug him and kiss his sweet face.
Star light, star bright,
First star I see tonight,
Please hold my wish to be true
Because I will see him once again but only in God's good time.
For I will always love that sweet angel of mine.

## THERE IS A BENCH THAT RESIDES ON THE CAMPUS OF UPSTATE

There is a bench that resides on the campus of Upstate.
The bench is engraved with the name of an athlete whose passion wa
running and who will always be remembered as a true Spartan.

The bench is strong and sturdy to withstand the test of time.
For it will always represent a courageous and brave soul
who strived to just finish the race of life.

The bench is nestled at the head of the Palmetto Trail.
For the bench will always and forever stand guard of the entrance wa
where runners will take refuge every day.

The bench will always be a symbol of a son, a friend, a class mate, a
student, a teammate, an athlete, and a person who walked upon and
ran on the hills of Upstate.

The bench will give rest to the weary and be a place for a moment of
peace and escape reality if only for a while.
Just sit quietly and patiently and you will feel a heavenly presence by
your side. It will be a runner who will always be your heavenly guide
There is a bench that resides on the campus of Upstate.

# CHAPTER EIGHTEEN
## *Just Finish the Race*

I deliver my first testimony on *Just Finish the Race* in front of 500 people at First Baptist Church of Cowpens on March 6, 2016. I am not one bit nervous.

I begin my testimony with the CNN video and give a detailed account of the events of the accident. I share how Johnny and I had to remove Josh from life support and I talk about the candlelight vigil and the funeral. I describe Josh's life and his legacy, and finally the dash. I describe Josh from birth until the last time we saw him. As I am speaking, the church is filled with the roar of laughter and the sounds of sobbing. I cry as I read my own poems, which are my refuge and an outlet to express my pain and grief. I believe that sharing them with others may help someone else who is grieving. The words of my poems don't come from a stranger's heart. The words come from a grieving mother's heart.

My nursing experience told me that my baby was badly hurt when I saw Josh lying in that hospital bed. But, as his mother, my heart was split into and part of my heart died the moment Josh died. My strength to get up every morning and face the world comes by God himself. Faced with the death of a child, trivial things in life no longer matter.

I have to speak for Josh. The words come to me with my poetry and in the night. The words seem to float into my mind and appear like a movie reel. Our memories will help us keep Josh alive in our hearts. We will keep him alive for others. I have to give this testimonial to preserve Josh's legacy. Sharing memories of Josh over and over again will guarantee Josh will never be forgotten. I will share stories about his childhood, teen years, and young adult life with generations to come. Why? Because Josh lived!

Josh was born August 13, 1995 at 8:20 a.m. He was a beautiful and good baby. Throughout his days here on Earth, Josh was always on the go. His exuberance for life touched the hearts of all who knew Josh. From the moment he woke up until he fell asleep, Josh loved, Josh laughed, and Josh lived everyday like it was his last.

As days, weeks and months pass, we received more than 800 sympathy cards and letters from friends and total strangers from across the country who heard about Josh's amazing life in the media. Coach Smith's interview where she describes Josh as a student and an athlete was featured on CNN and shown across the country. The story of Josh, James, Mills and Sarah captivated our community and others across the nation. Four vibrant student athletes from USC Upstate killed in a tragic car accident in the small college town of Spartanburg, South Carolina was news that interested all media outlets.

As weeks turned into months, Johnny and I learned so much about our son. We had absolutely no clue about the amazing life that Josh led outside our home. We all feel life owes us something. To Josh, life was worth nothing unless he used it for God's work and mankind. What Josh put into life was far more important that what Josh got out of it. Josh never, ever saw the color of skin or social class. Josh had a true gift for identifying a person in need of a friend or someone to talk with.

"Josh was my guy. He was the go-to person. Josh was our guy," we were told over and over again.

"Just Finish the Race, the race of life," is a phrase Josh used to encourage others. "Never give up, just finish. Just finish the race," is what Josh would say to his fellow classmates, teammates and total strangers. It doesn't matter the life situation. As long as you give 100% of your heart and soul, you can accomplish anything. You just have to stay focused on Jesus Christ and your race will be won. Giving back or paying it forward is the key.

As a young child in elementary school Josh rarely got to enjoy recess. Every day when he came home from school, I would ask him, "Josh, did you get recess today?"

"No, Mama. I had to help my friend or talk to them," was Josh's usual response.

He knew he would lose his recess but, he didn't care because he wanted to help his classmates. Josh made good grades and completed his work on time but his desire to help others meant more to him than any recess break. Johnny and I tried in earnest to make Josh understand that he could not get up in school or talk. Finally we gave up and quit fighting this losing battle with him. We knew Josh meant well and as long as his grades remained good we stopped pushing the issue with him.

Josh was a fierce, fierce friend who was loyal. Josh strived to invest his time in others because he cared so much about humanity. Finishing the race means you live by example, inspiring others to do so. Josh supported all athletics at Upstate. Several of the athletes from different sports told us that Josh would be in the stands cheering for the Spartans. Josh was a true Spartan at heart. During track and cross country meets or other sporting venues at Broome and Upstate his fellow teammates elaborated that Josh would be running along beside them or cheering from the stands or sidelines encouraging them not to give up. They said Josh would be screaming, "You've got this, don't quit. Push, push harder! Just finish the race!"

In an incredible tribute to Josh, Courtney, who played soccer at Upstate, and the cross country and track & field teams at Upstate wrote "Just Finish the Race" on their cleats or their legs when they were competing. Broome's football teams wore the #24 JRL, in memory of Josh, on their football helmets to pay homage to one of their own.

"Son, doesn't it make you mad that you are not playing much," I asked Josh after a high school football game.

"No, Mama. I am on a team and being on this team encouraging my teammates means more to me than any playing time," he told me with the biggest smile, which caused me to lose the attitude about Josh not playing and I cheered alongside of him from the stands.

Not long after Josh's funeral, Johnny and I received a letter from a soccer player in Oregon. He had traveled to Spartanburg and stopped by White's Pine Street Exxon one night when Josh was working. They discussed the World Cup and Josh was so excited about going to his friend's apartment to watch the game. The gentleman saw the news of Josh's death on CNN and felt he needed to write to us. He told us about how Josh changed his live in only the few minutes he spent with him. He went into detail about Josh's exuberance and being so full of life. Because of Josh, this man is trying to live everyday like it is his last.

We received a packet from one of Josh's classes at Upstate. The professor and each student wrote us a letter about how Josh made a difference in their lives. One letter in particular that touched my heart was from a young gentleman who has been bullied all his life. He was always the last one picked for a team or completely ignored. Their class had to complete a group project and the professor asked the class to choose teams. The young man wrote that Josh came up to him and grabbed his arm and said, 'Want you be on my team today?" The young man was so grateful to Josh because he was considering committing suicide and he had God to show him that he mattered. Because Josh befriended him and genuinely cared for his well-being, this young man is now standing up for himself and choosing to live and to finish his own race in life. He said Josh changed his life that day and he wanted Johnny and me to know that our son was sent to him from a higher being and he will be forever grateful to Josh.

A friend of Macy's who is in the Marines, learned of Josh's death on social media and had a disabled civilian in the Middle East paint a breathtaking portrait of Josh running with angels wings. She told Macy that even across the world; Josh's legacy was being shared because of the life he led. Grant, a friend of Josh's who is a Marine too, had an official military grade bracelet made with the inscription "Just Finish The Race" that he wears in memory of Josh.

"I can look down at it and remember to just finish, just finish the race and not to ever give up like Josh always did on daily basis," Grant told us.

Josh had been doing his student teaching at Spartanburg Christian Academy and we received letters from some of the teachers and students that knew him. They felt they needed to write us to tell us how much they had fallen in love with Josh because of Josh being Josh. They explained that Josh was constantly encouraging the kids to not ever give up. Josh was being a "kid" with them. Getting down upon their level, all the while, making them smile and bringing joy to their lives. They said it was rewarding to have him there even if it was just a short period of time because Josh was such a blessing to everyone at their school.

Courtney shared at the funeral that Josh Tweeted in March of 2015, "I do not want my presence known but my absence felt." His absence is felt by so many people and his story will be forever remembered by others by his example of life and his love for his faith, for which he shared often. The irony of this story is that Josh received the Lord Jesus Christ, as his savoir, as a tween with Macy at the Judgment House at Cudd Baptist Church in Spartanburg, S.C. The skit, according to Macy, was how a group of five friends all died in a motor vehicle accident, the exact same way Josh died 11 years later. My son knew he had Jesus Christ in his heart. Do You? If not, it is time to accept him because you are not promised tomorrow.

I was asked one day, "Why are you doing this?" It is a simple answer and I responded with a big smile on my face, 'It is for you."

Josh inspired others to do their best even if they came in last, you finished. How inspiring is this for a 20-year old to lift up his friends and family but mostly, total strangers? Josh never saw people by the color of their skin or social class. He had the ability to see within their hearts and souls. Josh had you at hello. His laughter and smile were contagious. His random burst into song or dance captured you because of his enthusiasm. If our testimony saves one life or brings another closer to the Lord then it is my responsibility to finish Josh's race. I truly believe I have been called to share *Just Finish the Race* and DUI awareness to anyone who will give me a chance.

# 365

It's been 365 days since God called your name and took you away.
365 days without seeing your handsome face.
365 days without looking into your baby blues.
365 days without being drawn into your contagious smile.
365 days without hearing your voice call my name.
365 days without hearing you telling your jokes.
365 days of hearing your rendition of Amazing Grace.
365 days without having your bear hugs.
365 days without saying sleep sweet and goodnight.
365 days without touching your bearded face and feeling the softness
of your skin.
365 days without rubbing my hand through your blond hair.
365 days without holding your hand when you were sick.
365 days without your Jethro bowl of cereal less than an hour after you
ate supper.
365 days without holding on to your arm for balance.
365 days without watching your own versions of line dancing.
365 days without seeing you drive around in your black Chevy truck.
365 days without seeing you squinting up your nose while you concen-
trate on your homework.
365 days without seeing you with the love of your life.
365 days without seeing you stare into Courtney's eyes in
total awe of her.
365 days without seeing you in your Upstate jersey.
365 days without your smelly socks and uniforms.
365 days without your messy room.
365 days without you displaying your love for mankind
regardless of color.
365 days without your encouragement for others to finish their race.
365 days without your calls or text that always ended with
I love you too Mama.
365 days just without you.

# CHAPTER NINETEEN
## A Year Later

### 365

The year 2016 taught us the true meaning of life with a new journey for us to travel. Johnny, Macy, and I had to learn to live without our Josh by our sides. Every single day our hearts would break when we looked at his portrait because we know now he is never coming home.

We have learned the true meaning of Thanksgiving and giving back. We established a scholarship at USC Upstate as our way of paying it forward. The scholarship has brought joy into our lives. To see a student smile and to be so grateful for our gift so they can finish their own race is rewarding.

We look upon life situations now with a smirk. There is no life drama or life situation that will ever compare to the loss of a child. Nothing! It isn't worth the effort. We blow off the little things now that use to upset or stress us. Life is too short to worry about the little things.

We have also been taught to never take life for granted. Just love unconditionally, just laugh every day, and just live every day like it is your last. To give thanks to God for every day you are given because your life can end in a split second. Death doesn't discriminate. It saddens us when we hear of a young person dying from car accidents, suicide, or medical and health issues.

We would have never imagined we would be grieving and fighting for justice for Josh. The South Carolina Attorney General agreed that toxicology reports are part of an individual's medical record and releasing them would violate the HIPPA laws. But, on February 29, 2016 the Spartanburg County Coroner did release the toxicology results to the public because he is not considered a medical professional and the HIPPA law does not apply to any coroner's office. So, the results were released and the chaos began all over again but finally, the rumors of Josh being an underage drinker stopped.

We are more aware of the triggers that bring the overwhelming pain of grief to our hearts. The moment it hits we have to let it play out. Grief doesn't care where you are or who you are with. It has to be dealt with on one's own time. There is no reasoning with grief.

We have been taught to truly look at others through our son's eyes. Josh saw everyone as equals and he loved unconditionally. This is a blessing from above. Johnny and I both work with the public but, in different circumstances. I know in my heart I have treated everyone equally and Johnny has too.

We have grown closer to God. We have truly changed as people. We love deeper because the cross is our only passage way to see Josh again. Josh is our guardian angel now. But, our relationship with God has grown. Yes, we get mad at God when the grief returns and He expects us too. But, knowing

Josh is on his right side of God, at the throne, enables me to push harder to build a stronger relationship with Him.

We have been taught the true meaning of forgiveness. We had to forgive God for taking Josh. We had to forgive James for his actions. But mostly, we had to learn to forgive Josh. Holding onto anger will destroy your spirit and soul. Forgiveness is a strong and emotional word. It was hard to forgive. But, the anger was eating us alive. It was hard to let the word escape my mouth but, once I said, "I forgive you," the weight lifted off my shoulders and my conscience became clear. It enabled us to move on and attempt to enjoy life again.

The year 2016 was also a year of first for us. First holidays, birthdays, vacations, and favorite restaurants without our son was extremely hard to manage. But, we learned that reminiscing helped us heal. The memories mostly brought tears but we have seemed to find a story where Josh made us laugh.

The year 2017 is another journey for us. It will be a journey that we, as separate individuals, have to cross by ourselves. Johnny, Macy, and I will participate in a different race on a daily basis. All we can do is never give up. Just finish, just finish the race of life. Josh did!

In the book of 2 Timothy 4:7, "I have fought the good fight, I have finished the race, I have kept the faith." (NIV) Josh was an inspiring Christian who loved life but, more importantly Josh never wavered with his faith. Josh's dates for living until death are August 13, 1995 – October 11, 2015. It is the dash that represents your life and accomplishment. Our Josh accomplished more in his 20 years of life than most do in 100 years of life. He loved, he laughed, and he brought happiness, friendship and laughter into everything and everyone who had the pleasure to meet or know him. So the question is, what is your dash going to represent? What do you want to get out of life, but more importantly WHAT are you going put into it?? Just finish your own race. Whether you are fighting a disease, competing in an athletic event, dealing with a trying life situation, or just having a bad day, JUST FINSH THE RACE! Maybe this is my race to tell Joshua's story to the world. What will be yours?

*Photo by: Matthew Johnson, USC-Upstate*

## JUST FINISH THE RACE

You ran with your teammates the grassy hills of the Upstate.
You ran with your teammates on top of the Appalachian Mountains.
You ran with your teammates on the sandy shores of the coast.
Son, you finished your race.
You gave strength to those who were weak.
You gave friendship to those who were lonely.
You gave love to all of mankind, regardless of color.
Son, you finished your race.
You encouraged the sick to fight for the cure.
You encouraged the young to stand up and be heard.
You encouraged the mentally and physically challenged
to persevere.
Son, you finished your race.
You brought laughter to the sad.
You brought smiles to the shy.
You brought love to everyone unconditionally.
Son, you finished your race.
You are now in Heaven running the streets of gold.
You are now everyone's guardian angel with your wings of white.
Your light is now the brightest star of all.
For this we vow our Son
we will, "Just Finish the Race!"

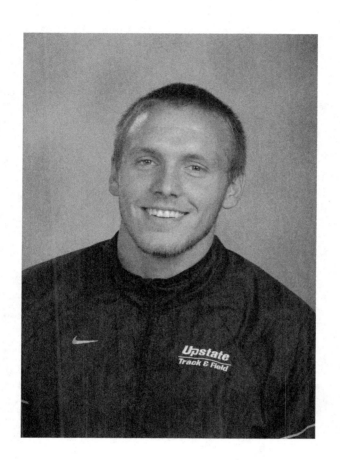

CPSIA information can be obtained
at www.ICGtesting.com
Printed in the USA
FSOW04n1810311217
42638FS